Their Light Still Shines

Inspiring Stories of Faith and Courage

Lewann Sotnak

Augsburg
MINNEAPOLIS

Dedicated to the memory of my mother, Astrid Dahle Awes, who supplied my childhood with countless stories about great men and women of faith.

THEIR LIGHT STILL SHINES
Inspiring Stories of Faith and Courage

Scripture quotations unless otherwise noted are from the New Revised Standard Version Bible, copyright © 1989 by the Division of Christian Education of the National Council of the Churches of Christ in the United States of America. Used with permission.

Interior design: Karen Buck
Cover design: Baker Group Design
Cover photo: FPG International

Library of Congress Cataloging-in-Publication Data
Sotnak, Lewann.
    Their light still shines : inspiring stories of faith and courage
/ Lewann Sotnak.
      p.   cm.
    ISBN 0-8066-2605-4 (alk. paper) :
    1. Christian biography.   I Title.
    BR1700.2.S68   1993
    270'.092'2—dc20
    [B]   93-36828
                                 CIP

The paper used in this publication meets the minimum requirements of American National Standard for Information Sciences—Permanence of Paper for Printed Library Materials, ANSI Z329.48-1984. ∞™

Manufactured in the U.S.A.   AF 9-2605

97   96   95   94   93   1   2   3   4   5   6   7   8   9   10

Contents

Acknowledgments   7

Introduction   9

1. Frank Laubach   11

2. Harriet Tubman   17

3. Toyohiko Kagawa   25

4. Jane Addams   32

5. Paul-Émile Léger   40

6. Marie Sandvik   47

7. William Booth   54

8. Catherine Mumford Booth   60

9. Robert Childress   66

10. Florence Nightingale   73

11. Robert Raikes   80

12. Elizabeth Fry   86

13. Pasha Tichomirow   92

14. Corrie and Betsie ten Boom   98

15. George Washington Carver   105

16. Dorothy Day   112

17. Sadhu Sundar Singh   119

18. Tariri   128

For Further Reading   133

Acknowledgments

A thank you to the following who provided information for this book:

Luther Northwestern Theological Seminary Library for their generous lending policies with inter-seminary loan services.

Portage Lake District Library in Houghton, Michigan, and Aitkin Public Library in Aitkin, Minnesota, for their efforts to secure materials through inter-library loans.

Lorrie Doris Anderson, a Wycliffe Bible translator and missionary who lived in Tariri's community in Peru. She read the chapter on Tariri and made valuable suggestions to correct inaccuracies or cultural misunderstandings.

Doris Nye who arranged an interview for me with Marie Sandvik a year before Marie's death. Doris and Marie also read the chapter on Marie Sandvik and provided a tour of the Marie Sandvik Center.

Pastor Robin Øye who introduced me to the name of Paul-Émile Cardinal Léger.

The Archdiocese in Montreal for newspaper articles on Paul-Émile Cardinal Léger.

The Canadian Conference of Catholic Bishops for providing material on Cardinal Léger.

Chantal Théorêt, Communications Coordinator at the Jules and Paul-Émile Léger Foundation in Québec who worked closely with Cardinal Léger, provided me with valuable books, and reviewed for accuracy the chapter about the Cardinal.

Felton Davis of the *New York Catholic Worker* and Peter Trebtoske of the Dorothy Day Center in St. Paul, Minnesota, for information on their organizations.

Larry Riddle who loaned me irreplaceable books of Sadhu Sundar Singh's writings, which were once owned by his missionary grandfather, T. E. Riddle, who knew the Sadhu in India.

Irene Getz, my editor at Augsburg Fortress, and production editor Stefanie Cox for their valuable insights.

And finally to my husband, Otto, for his endless patience in teaching me new wonders of what computers can do.

Introduction

The world desperately needs good news. At every turn, however, it seems that bad news dominates the media. It's broadcast on radio and television, printed in newspapers and magazines, and talked about in social circles. Yet, when evil seems to be gaining the upper hand, God often surprises us, working through steadfast followers and turning the darkness into light. This book tells the stories of people who have proclaimed the good news and carried the gospel's shining light into the world's dark and needy corners.

Throughout history and into the present, God's light-bearers have come from a variety of backgrounds and cultures. Their personalities have ranged from boisterous to quiet, timid to brash, mystical to practical. Some individuals are well known and colorful; others humble and unrenowned. They have by no means been perfect. Some have had personality flaws; made mistakes; shown poor judgment at times; or struggled with temptations, hot tempers, petty jealousies, arrogance, or resentment. In spite of human weakness we find hope when we remember that God uses faithful people with whatever gifts they have.

Groups or individuals tend to believe that they have an exclusive claim on God, and that their understanding of faith is superior to those with other perspectives. But people's views about life and God's role in their lives depend on a number of influences: their geographical locations, their cultural backgrounds, the individuals to whom they've been exposed, their childhood experiences, their own personalities, and the literature they have read.

With such a variety of individuals in the world, there must also be countless ways in which the light of Christ's love is passed on and hearts are touched. God comes to people in ways that are amazingly diverse.

This book describes nineteen believers who heard God's call and worked to make a difference in the world. These reports are as historically accurate as possible. Sources do not always agree in their descriptions of events. Figures who traveled and spoke frequently repeated their stories and ideas in slightly different ways, so some quotes differ from one source to another. Also, the events of history are recorded by writers who often interpret them in their own way, or whose descriptions have changed as they have been handed down by word of mouth.

The words spoken by the main characters in these chapters are either direct quotes or paraphrases from quotes in order to simplify them. Wherever possible, the main character's writings have been relied upon to create conversation. Some books have not listed their sources.

In a number of the chapters, imagination has created the conversations of minor people to add interest to the story, but the substance of their words is based on historical information.

1 *Frank Laubach*   1884–1970

Frank was discouraged. Why was he such a failure with the Moro people? Long ago he had made a vow to go where the need was greatest and to fight where the ranks were thinnest and the battle hottest. Now he struggled to fulfill that vow in Dansalan on Lake Lanao in the Philippines. But the natives were cold and hostile toward him and suspicious of his Christian religion.

Every evening, Frank climbed to his favorite spot at the top of Signal Hill. He came there to meditate and sort out the day's events. As Frank stretched out on the grass, he thought back to his keen disappointment in losing the election for the presidency of Union College and Theological Seminary in Manila where he had taught when he first came to these islands as a missionary. That loss still stung. At that time, Frank believed he was best suited for the job. The bitter part was that he lost the election by one vote, the one vote he himself cast for his opponent out of a generous heart.

The feelings of failure ate away at Frank until he realized his attitude was beginning to cause physical problems. If God had closed the door on the presidency, there must be something else he should do with his life. Why, then, was he failing in this new place?

Frank was not accustomed to failure. In the past he had experienced success in everything he did . . . in school as a youngster, in graduate school, seminary, social work in the slums, then in his missionary work and teaching. If God wanted him here, why were things not working out? He felt especially alone because for the time being, his wife, Effa, and their little son remained in Manila where it was safer.

The next day Frank took his basket and set off for the marketplace. Today he would try again to make friends and interest the Moros in starting a school. Sunlight filtered through the tall palm trees. He passed by people at work in their rice fields and coconut groves. A man rode past in a two-wheeled cart, drawn by a slow, wide-horned water buffalo. Frank waved and smiled at him, but he turned coldly away.

Laubach passed the ruins of a public high school. Five years ago a few native Christian teachers had acted indiscreetly toward some of the female students, and the pupils' angry fathers had retaliated by killing several teachers and burning schools to the ground. That ended formal education for many young girls. Because of this incident, the fear, suspicion, and hatred toward Christianity increased.

Frank despaired. What could make the difference? Didn't he have a great message of God's love to share? There must be some way to reach these Moros. He hoped to start a school again. Surely by this time the people would be interested in such a project.

Frank reached the marketplace. The odor of fish permeated the air. Women exchanged news of the day. Men conversed in groups as they chewed and spit betel nuts through blackened teeth. Some wore white pantaloons and coats with gold buttons. Daggers hung from their sashed tunics. Other shoppers wore bright-striped, handwoven robes. Dirty, muslin rags clothed the poorest of the crowd.

Frank bought sweet potatoes, bananas, and mangoes. The merchants failed to return his smile. He went into a dim, tiny shop that smelled of oil and sandalwood. A man in a turban was talking to the proprietor. They eyed Frank with hostility and talked in low voices. Frank looked over a lovely silver box, inlaid with ivory and set with precious stones. Suddenly the proprietor snatched up the box. "This is not for sale," he said brusquely, and carried it to a back room. Frank left and walked the streets. He tried to interest the Moros in a new school, but they turned away without answering him.

As the days went by, Frank's discouragement mounted. He prayed harder and meditated faithfully as he tried to find the solution to his problems with the Moro people. Each evening he climbed Signal Hill behind his cottage and watched the sun set. Picturesque mountains, lakes, and the distant sea stretched before his eyes. He sat absorbed in nature's beauty; he prayed and waited for an answer.

At this time Frank was also trying an experiment, which he hoped would help him deepen his spiritual life. He wanted to be conscious of

God every moment of every day, concentrating on God to direct his thoughts, his fingers, his steps, his words. This experiment was difficult.

As Frank made his usual climb up Signal Hill, he had no idea that he was about to face a new challenge. His little black dog, Tip, ran along, sniffing, barking, and chasing small animals into their holes or up trees. His tail wagged with freedom. Frank wished he could have a bit of that joy. At the top of the hill, he settled into his favorite spot to meditate. He begged God to help him reach the unreachable Moro people.

Suddenly Frank heard God, not in audible words, but in a powerful directive to his mind. "My child, you have failed because you do not really love these Moros. You feel superior to them because you are white. Forget you are an American, and think only of how I love them. They will respond."[1]

Frank Laubach was stunned by the truth of God's message. Was he so intent on himself and his own agenda with the Moros that he had been closed to God's leading? He admitted that he did think of the Moros as ignorant and dirty. He did not love them or what he saw in his own heart. He prayed to become empty of himself and open to God's spirit.

Again God spoke, "If you want the Moros to be fair to your religion, be fair to theirs. Study the Koran with them."[2]

A breakthrough! Frank rushed down the hill with Tip after him, excitement growing. The next day Laubach visited some panditas (priests) and told them that he wanted to study the Koran. The priests' eyes lit up. At last, they thought, this man was ready to become a good Muslim. They crowded into his cottage holding a pamphlet which listed their holy books of Islam. Frank read the titles: the Torah, the laws of Moses; the Zabur, the psalms of David; the Kitab Injil, the gospel of Jesus Christ; and the Koran of Muhammad. "I have read the first three books on your list all my life," he said. Here was common ground to share. Enthusiastically the discussion continued, exchanging ideas.

"I want to learn to read your Maranaw language, and also how to speak it better," Laubach told the priests. He knew that only then could he talk in depth with the people.

"But not a single page of our language has ever been written down," the priests told him. "The Koran and our other holy books are written in Arabic, and this is too difficult for most of our people to learn."

An opportunity for Laubach! He knew he must learn Maranaw better himself; then he could devise a method of writing the language so it would be easy to teach others to read it. An ex-convict, Dato Pambaya, became his tutor. As he studied, Laubach and an assistant also began working on a dictionary, using Roman letters. It was tedious work because no one knew where one Maranaw word ended and another began. The language seemed to be one long, run-on word.

Laubach learned more than language from Pambaya. "A good Muslim ought to say the sacred word for God every time he begins to do anything, to sleep, or walk, or work, or even turn around. A good Muslim's life will be filled with God, though I fear there are few good Muslims."[3]

"A Christlike Christian will do the same," said Laubach, "though I fear there are few good Christians."[4]

As Laubach worked, the native village buzzed with expectation. "Come see what Mr. Laubach is doing. He is writing a dictionary in *our* language!" the people told each other. They constantly interrupted Laubach's work, "We are so grateful to you. No one ever tried to understand us before you came."

Frank was patient with the interruptions. He shared with the people his experiment of trying to keep God in his consciousness every moment of every day. "You are being just like Mohammed," they said. "You teach us beautiful things from the Koran."

"But I learned these things from Jesus," Frank answered. As Laubach began appreciating the wisdom and beauty of the Koran, the Moros began to see that there were also wise and beautiful teachings in the Christian Bible. They also saw that this missionary lived what he taught!

As Frank worked, he often hummed a childhood hymn.

Moment by moment I'm kept in his love;
Moment by moment, I've life from above;
Looking to Jesus till glory doth shine;
Moment by moment, O Lord, I am Thine.[5]

Laubach had ups and downs with his spiritual experiment. Some weeks were complete failures, but he found that as he searched to know God more fully, new insights were revealed. He realized that as one makes new discoveries about friends by being with them, so it was with God. "I must talk about God, or I cannot keep him in my mind,"[6] Laubach wrote to his father. "If we are so impoverished that we have nothing to reveal but small talk, then we need to struggle for more richness of soul."[7]

In Laubach's work, surprising developments began to unfold. The Muslim panditas, or priests, who had often encouraged rebellions in various areas, sent word to those places to stop the fighting. Residents from one conflict-torn area asked that Laubach help them start a school. An outlaw brought Frank a copy of the New Testament and requested one in his own Maranaw language so he could study it. Two leading Muslim priests were impressed by the missionary's example and began telling people around the province, "Mr. Laubach can help us to know God."

A local merchant offered Laubach a former dance hall and theater for a school. Someone from another city sent a printing press, complete with a printer to operate it. When the machine arrived, Laubach discovered a slab of concrete on the floor of the old building that he was converting into the new school. It was just the right size to support the thousand-pound printing press.

When the first newspaper appeared, crowds of people begged to learn reading. Through trial and error, Laubach simplified his reading charts until the people experienced immediate success. After one session, an outlaw told Laubach, "You're the best friend I have because you taught me to read. Now I want to do you a favor." His voice dropped to a whisper, "Is there anybody in Lanao you want me to put out of the way?"

"No, thank you, brother," said Laubach. "I don't want that. But you certainly are a big-hearted man. What you can do for me is to go home to your village and teach someone else. That would make me happy," Laubach responded.[8]

By the time Effa joined her husband with their son, much of the antagonism toward Christianity had dwindled. Just as things were going well and hundreds of new people were learning to read, the depression struck in the United States, and missionary funds dried up. With anguish, Laubach called in his dozen paid teachers one by one and told them, "It would be easier for me to jump into the lake than to face you with the news that you can no longer be paid."[9] When the teachers saw Laubach's own distress, all who could possibly afford it volunteered to continue teaching without pay, and within a month the number of volunteers had risen to 175.

By this time an important local leader, Chief Kakai Dagalangit, had heard about the lack of resources. He had seen the value in literacy and wanted the program to continue. He came to Laubach and said, "This campaign must not stop because we have no money. It is our only hope for Lanao. Therefore, each one who learns how to read must teach someone else. If he doesn't, I shall kill him!"

Although Laubach was a bit amused at the vehement leader, he was suddenly energized by the idea, which came to be known as "each one teach one." Not only would it help the ones who were learning, but it would create a sense of pride and self-respect in those who were teaching.

Before long the "each one teach one" motto became the driving force behind the reading campaign. The idea spread like wildfire all over the islands. Soon leaders from countries in every part of the world asked Dr. Frank Laubach to come help them set up reading programs. Throughout all the hectic hours of work and travel, Laubach still took time to meditate and pray that he would live within God's will every moment of every day.

As he thought about his past struggle with the Moro people, Dr. Laubach said, "What right have I or any other person to come here and change the name of these people from Muslim to Christian, unless I lead them to a life fuller of God than they have now? Clearly, clearly, my job here is not to go to the town plaza and make proselytes; it is to *live* wrapped in God, trembling to his thoughts, burning with his passion. I do not have to wait until some future time for the glorious hour. I need not sing, 'Oh that will be glory for me—' and wait for any grave. *This hour* can be heaven. *Any* hour for *any* body can be as rich as God!"[10]

Notes

1. Marjorie Medary, *Each One Teach One* (New York: David McKay Company, 1954), 31.

2. Ibid., 31.

3. Frank C. Laubach, *Letters by a Modern Mystic* (New York: Student Volunteer Movement, 1937), 14–15.

4. Ibid., 15.

5. Daniel W. Whittle, words; May Whittle Moody, music; the Billy Graham Team, compilers, "Moment by Moment," #184, *Crusader Hymns and Hymn Stories* (Minneapolis: The Billy Graham Evangelistic Association, 1966–67).

6. Laubach, *Modern Mystic,* 25.

7. Ibid., 11.

8. Medary, *Each One,* 39.

9. Ibid., 44.

10. Laubach, *Modern Mystic,* 15.

2 *Harriet Tubman*   ca. 1820–1913

An overseer stood watch, ready to whip any slave who rested for even a moment or who visited with another worker. But today a frightening message was whispered to Harriet in the fields. "I've heard you are to be sold into the deep South tonight!" Never could Harriet forget seeing her two sisters marched off in a chain gang with ropes tied about their wrists and ankles, one leaving crying children behind.

Harriet's mind reeled as the new fear enveloped her. For years she had dreamed day and night of escaping to the North. From here in Maryland there was a chance to succeed, but escaping from the deep South would be nearly impossible. She must go *now*! Besides, with her sleeping spells, she wouldn't survive the march.

The strange spells had begun with a head injury received when Harriet was in her teens. She had blocked an overseer in a store so he couldn't catch a runaway slave. The overseer grabbed an iron weight and threw it after the retreating slave but it struck Harriet on the forehead instead. For months her mother nursed her as she hovered near death. When she finally recovered, a deep scar remained as well as an injury to her brain, which caused her to fall asleep without warning.

During that time of illness Harriet had begun to pray constantly. First her prayers were, "Lord, convert Old Master." When he tried to sell her, her prayers changed to, "Lord, if you're not going to convert him, kill him."[1] When her master died suddenly, Harriet was so guilt-ridden that she said she would give the whole world full of gold to bring his soul back.[2]

Tubman's prayer life continued in her recovery. When she swept she prayed God to sweep away her sin. When she washed or watered the horses, she asked God to wash her heart clean.[3] As she prayed for freedom, she began to realize that she must help answer that prayer herself.

For years Harriet had heard about the Underground Railroad, a secret route to the North, with "conductors" along the way who were willing to help slaves escape. Many of these conductors were Quakers who believed it was against God's law for anyone to call another person "master." It still seemed incredible to Harriet that white people would risk their own safety to help black people. She remembered hearing: "You can always trust the Quakers. They're almost as good as colored folk." Recently a Quaker woman had given Harriet detailed directions and a note to bring to her first conductor if she decided to run away.

Harriet knew the risks. When a slave vanished, handbills were distributed immediately and signs posted. Slave catchers took to their horses and bloodhounds joined in the search. Cruel punishment awaited anyone who was caught.

Even so, nothing could hold Harriet back. "I reasoned this out in my mind. There are two things I have a right to, liberty or death. If I can't have one, I'll have the other. I'll fight for my liberty as long as my strength lasts, and when the time comes for me to go, the Lord will let them take me."[4] If she survived her escape, once she learned the route with all its hiding places, she would come back and rescue others.

Just then the overseer's horn sounded across the field. The long day's work was over. There was no time to lose. First Harriet needed to let family and friends know that when she disappeared, she had not been sold. She walked by the big house where her sister was working, then past the slave cabins. In her beautiful contralto voice she sang: "I'm sorry I'm going to leave you. Farewell, oh farewell, . . . I'll meet you in the morning. Safe in the promised land . . ."[5] Slaves often passed along information by singing songs that concealed messages.

Next Harriet threw supplies into her ticking bag, grabbed the cherished patchwork quilt she had sewn herself, and set out in the moonlight for the Quaker woman's house. She left the quilt in the door as a thank you, then plunged through the fields and into the woods, keeping alert for every danger.

Harriet passed the old oak tree where the slaves used to worship together and hear stories about Moses leading the Israelites to freedom. Since a slave uprising, new laws decreed that slaves could no longer meet unless a white was present, so after that they met secretly in the woods. No slave was allowed to beat a drum, blow a horn, or be out on the roads without a pass. Anyone caught teaching a slave to read faced life imprisonment or death. Even the Bible was banned in slave quarters, as well as Harriet's favorite song, "Go Down Moses . . . Let my people go."

Harriet remembered a literate slave reading a report on these laws from a smuggled newspaper at a secret meeting. A Virginia legislator declared, "We have as far as possible closed every avenue by which light may enter slaves' minds. If we could extinguish the capacity to see the light our work would be completed; they would then be on a level with the beasts of the field."[6]

A screech owl startled Harriet. "Head for the Choptank River," her Quaker friend had told her. "Then follow it." Harriet had memorized every direction. She pressed forward through woods, marshes, oozy swamps, over logs, and under branches. Tangled briars and thorns tore her skin and hair. Sometimes she waded waist-deep in water so the bloodhounds could not pick up her scent. "I'm going to hold steady unto you, Lord, and you've got to see me through," she prayed.[7]

She had to go as far as possible that first night before the alarm went out for her capture. On and on she marched toward the North Star and freedom.

Finally Harriet's feet would move no more. She ate some soggy bread and cold pork, then dropped exhausted into the hollow of an old tree. Dreams mingled with memories. Years ago, when she was only five, she went to work for Miss Susan.

"Dust the furniture!" Miss Susan ordered. Slave cabins had no furniture, so Harriet didn't know how to dust. Miss Susan whipped her about the face and neck until welts rose on her skin. She whipped her if the baby cried, and once she whipped her four times before breakfast.[8] Again and again the whip came down on her tender flesh. Harriet awoke in a panic, and Miss Susan's hateful face faded. She remembered her own mother who always treated her children gently because she believed the world was harsh enough.

By this time the sun was high. Harriet started out again and traveled on until dark when she reached the highway. She had to cross fifteen miles of open fields next. Suddenly she heard hoof beats. Dropping into a ditch, she pressed close to the ground. A few men stopped just a few feet away to build a fire. While they ate supper and drank corn whiskey their talk grew louder. "She can't have gotten too far," one said.

"We'll get her yet!" added another.

Harriet's heart beat wildly. When the men galloped away, Harriet hurried on, weak from terror. She made wide circles around each farm lest a barking dog give her away. At midnight she dragged her weary feet into the town of Camden and made her way to a Quaker home, the Ezekiel Hunn house. "Ezekiel takes people in day or night," she had been told. How good a real bed would feel right now . . . But something warned Harriet to wait for morning. To keep awake she circled around in a nearby field.

In the morning a Quaker woman dressed in gray came out and began to sweep. Harriet brought her the note. The woman hardly glanced at it, but thrust the broom at her. "Sweep!" she ordered, and hurried into the house. Harriet swept, ready to run if this proved to be a trap.

Finally a Quaker man and his guest came out. The guest mounted his chestnut mare and galloped away. When his hoofbeats were far away, the Quaker man said to Harriet: "Thee are most welcome here. I am Ezekiel Hunn. That man was a slave trader. He wanted to buy some hay from me so he stopped for the night."

Harriet shuddered. She had almost knocked during the night! Ezekiel invited her into the pleasant home where Mrs. Hunn served a tasty meal. Harriet thought of all the good food she had seen at her master's table but was forbidden to eat because she was a slave. She even had been flogged when she was only seven for tasting a sugar lump.

After a long rest, Ezekiel hitched up the team and by night drove Harriet to Smyrna. "I must be back before dawn because the patrols are watching me too," he said. He described her route and told her how to find the home of his brother John in Middletown.

Hours of dangerous travel brought Harriet to John Hunn's home. After food and rest, John warned, "Wilmington is where thee must go next, but the border, bridges, and road both to and from the city are heavily guarded at all times. Thee must have an escort. I cannot take thee because if the authorities see my carriage by Thomas Garrett's place, he and I will be arrested." John gave Harriet careful directions and drove her the first twenty-three miles. "Be extra careful from here on."

Harriet stumbled through the dark night until she had one of her sleeping spells. Abruptly she awoke to a whinny. Close by, men on horses were talking. Harriet flattened herself against a tree trunk. One man said, "She must have been let off near Smyrna. Someone saw Hunn's carriage returning from there."

"It's too dark to see anything without the moon," added another. "Let's give up for now. She's sure to be headed for Wilmington. We'll find her there in the morning."

The men galloped off toward Wilmington. Harriet, still shaking, continued on cautiously, keeping her distance from the road. Thick fog made travel difficult.

As she approached Wilmington, she picked her way up a rocky slope to the cemetery John had described and fell among the tombstones, exhausted. Within a few minutes she felt a gentle tap. She reached for her hunting knife. "I am a conductor and I bring you a ticket for the railroad," said a voice. Harriet knew she was safe.

The man gave Harriet a suit of men's clothes, a cap, and a rake. Together the pair walked across the bridge, past guards and patrollers. No one paid any attention to the two Negro men on their way to "work."

At Thomas Garrett's house Harriet was hustled upstairs to a secret room behind a bookcase in the wall. Thomas whispered, "Thee must hide here and be very quiet. My shoestore is underneath. There are handbills everywhere, advertising thy escape."

For two days Tubman hid. On First Day (Sunday) when everyone was in church, the Garretts gave Harriet new shoes, her washed and mended clothes, and a disguise. Then Thomas drove her by carriage to the outskirts of Wilmington and pointed out the route. "Only about eight more miles to the Pennsylvania border. There will be signposts between Delaware and Pennsylvania," he said. "When you pass the signs thee will be free." He pressed a silver dollar in her hand.

Harriet half ran, and half walked along the path until she reached the border. The journey had taken almost a week. Cautiously she peeked out from bushes and hedges, but she saw no one. She wished she could read the sign, but it looked just as Thomas Garrett had described it. She crossed the line into the free zone.

Free at last! Harriet wanted to shout and sing, but instead the tears flowed. Later she told her friends, "I looked at my hands to see if I was the same person now I was free. There was such a glory over everything. The sun came like gold through the trees and over the fields and I felt like I was in Heaven."[9]

Harriet was free, but this was only the beginning. "I had crossed the line," she said later. "I was free; but there was no one to welcome me to the land of freedom. I was a stranger in a strange land."[10] She believed that as long as there was one slave left, that made her a slave too.

Harriet went back nineteen times into the South and brought more than three hundred slaves to freedom. In order to support herself and raise money to finance her rescue missions, Harriet cooked, cleaned, washed laundry, worked in hotels, and grew and sold vegetables.

In 1850 the Fugitive Slave Law was passed, which required runaway slaves to be returned to their masters—even those who had already escaped and established homes in the North. They were denied a jury trial, so many of Harriet's "passengers" had to travel another thousand miles into Canada.

One of Harriet's rescue trips was the spectacular deliverance of her aged parents. Such a feat was called "a diabolical act of wickedness and cruelty," by John Bell Robinson, a vigorous supporter of slavery. He declared, "Confinement in the penitentiary for life would be 'inadequate' to her crime, for stealing her old parents away from a good home and friends, and a living already laid out sufficient for all their wants . . ."[11]

Harriet's journeys took her through ice, snow, pouring rain, and many dangers. She fed babies paregoric to keep them quiet. Railroad "conductors" transported her parties in wagons under bricks and vegetables, hid them in potato holes, swamps, and haystacks. To ensure the safety of all her charges, Harriet's word was law. "Move or die," she told recalcitrant travelers, threatening them with a gun. "Dead slaves tell no tales."

Many white people and free blacks risked their lives and property to help the slaves escape. Thomas Garrett of the Wilmington shoe store fed, clothed, and sheltered twenty-five hundred runaway slaves. When he was brought to trial for these misdeeds, his fines for damages took his every last dollar. All his possessions were sold at a public auction. The sheriff who conducted the sale said to Garrett, "Thomas, I hope you'll never be caught at this again."

Sixty-year-old Garrett replied, "Friend, I haven't a dollar in the world, but if thee knows a fugitive anywhere on the face of the earth who needs a breakfast, send him to me."[12]

Harriet became known as Moses to people everywhere. She had many close calls. Once friends found her sleeping under a sign that advertised a $40,000 reward for her capture.

Another time she heard two men talking about her as she rode a train. She pulled a book out of her bag and pretended to read. One of the men said, "Oh that can't be her. The one we want can't read." Harriet said later, "And I was only praying I had the book right side up."[13]

During the Civil War Harriet served as a spy for the Union Army. Her missions took her deep into the South where she knew the routes and was well loved among slaves on nearly every plantation. Many slave owners underestimated both the intelligence of their slaves and their desire for freedom, and they often discussed critical information in front of them. This they passed on to Harriet. These facts enabled Harriet to lead many successful raids, which earned her the title of General Tubman.

Harriet also organized much-needed medical care on the front lines. She cared for both black and white soldiers. She directed her staff to scrub, mop, and clean the premises and repair broken equipment. She battled with the War Department offices until she received medical supplies and the promise of more doctors. Appointed matron of the hospital, she brought order out of chaos.

After an exhausting day of work, Harriet would go home to sleep a few hours, then bake pies and cakes to sell so she could support herself because she had too much pride to beg. When disease epidemics broke out, she gathered herbs and roots and made traditional slave medicines. Numerous soldiers were cured by Harriet's remedies after the doctors had given up on them.

Finally Harriet decided to go to her home in Albany, N.Y., and rest. As the train pulled away from Washington, D.C., she dozed until a conductor rudely shouted at her. "You can't sit here. No Negroes allowed. Get in the baggage car." Harriet refused. She had fought the war and risked her life for men like him. The conductor called on others to "help get the nigger out." Three more men carried her from her seat and threw her into the baggage car, causing her to wrench her shoulder. Harriet was hurt more in soul than in body. "All those years of fighting and never a scratch from a Rebel sword or gun. Had to wait till I was coming home to get my first war wound," she muttered.[14]

Harriet was never able to collect the military pay she should have received for her services. She had financial problems all her life because she gave away most of her resources. Her small home in Auburn, N. Y., was always open to the needy. Despite her limited income, she stymied her brother by bidding on twenty-five acres of rich farmland including buildings, which she wanted to buy as a home for the poor, old, and homeless.

When her brother asked her how she was going to pay for the property, Harriet said, "Don't you worry. After telling the Lord Jesus about it, I'm going to the bank. . . . Bank'll give me a mortgage and lend me the money, sure."[15] And it did. Eventually she deeded the property over to the African Methodist Episcopal Zion Church.

Looking back at Harriet's Underground Railroad activities, people marveled at her uncanny sense of knowing when to advance, when to retreat, where to hide, and how to trick her captors. When asked how she did it, she answered, "It's the Lord." She prayed faithfully and left the results to God. She said, "On my Underground Railroad, I never ran my train off the track, and I never lost a passenger."[16]

Notes

1.   Earl Conrad, *Harriet Tubman, A Biography* (New York: Paul S. Eriksson, 1943), 19.

2.   Ibid., 20.

3.   Ibid., 19.

4.   Ibid., 36.

5.   Ibid., 37.

6.   Dorothy Sterling, *Freedom Train: The Story of Harriet Tubman* (New York: Doubleday & Co., 1954), 37.

7.   Ann Petry, *Harriet Tubman: Conductor on the Underground Railroad* (New York: Pocket Books, 1955), 205.

8.   Conrad, *Biography,* 8.

9.   Ibid., 38.

10.   Ibid., 40.

11.   Ibid., 99–100.

12.   Petry, *Conductor,* 51.

13.   Sterling, *Freedom Train,* 121.

14.   Ibid., 167.

15.   Ibid., 173.

16.   Ibid., 179.

3 *Toyohiko Kagawa* 1888–1960

"Toyohiko! You're wanted on the athletic field immediately." Although the student who brought the message sounded business-like, a tiny smirk made Toyohiko uneasy. Why would anyone want to see him on the field at this hour of the day?

Toyohiko Kagawa followed the student out of the dormitory and along the main path. They didn't speak to each other on the way. Kagawa knew that both faculty and students in this Presbyterian college in Tokyo considered him odd. He was a prodigious writer and a reader of all the books and literature in the library, and he frequently, though unintentionally, embarrassed his professors by knowing more than they did.

It was his ideas, however, that made him unpopular. Since becoming a Christian, he believed he must take the words and teachings of Jesus literally. He openly opposed his own government's international policies, its attack on Russia, and the increasing development of militarism and nationalism. Kagawa knew the whole college sided against him, but hadn't Jesus died on the cross rather than resisting those who hated him?

Kagawa followed as his guide turned off the main path. Where was he going, anyhow? Suddenly a group of students leaped out from behind a clump of shrubs and attacked him. "Dirty traitor!" they yelled. "Russian lover! Enemy of the people! Coward! We'll beat that pacifism out of you." Fists and feet flailed as Toyohiko was beaten, kicked, punched, and scratched.

Toyohiko felt the blood running down his face. He tasted it, mixed with the dirt as it ground into his teeth. When the attack was over, Toyohiko lay still. Searing pain shot through his body. He struggled with the anger and humiliation he felt. Weren't his ancestors the *samurai* who never forgave anyone for injury? But now he lived under a new law, and a new leader, Jesus, the forgiving Savior of all races.

Slowly Toyohiko rose up on his knees. His body shook with the shock of the beating. He clasped his hands together and called out, "Father, forgive them. They know not what they do."[1] One by one the attackers slunk away without a word. What kind of person was this Toyohiko Kagawa, anyhow?

Not only did Kagawa's pacifism set him apart, but also his concern for the poor, suffering, and despised of society. His roommates never knew what to expect. One day they returned to their quarters to find a mangy dog Toyohiko had rescued. Another time he brought home a starving kitten. The next surprise was a beggar covered with sores, resting on Kagawa's bed. Finally the college authorities put a stop to such unappetizing mercy.

Orphaned at four, Toyohiko had grown up in a harsh home without love. He learned English from two Presbyterian missionaries, Dr. Charles A. Logan and Dr. Harry W. Myers, and experienced in their homes the love he had always longed for. Kagawa said, "It is not the Bible alone which has taught me what Christianity means, but the love of these two homes."[2] Stories of Jesus moved him to tears, and when he became a Christian in his teens, he prayed, "Oh God, make me like Christ."[3] This started him on the hazardous journey that influenced all the decisions of his life.

It was on Christmas Eve, 1909, that Toyohiko carried out a decision that everyone considered ludicrous. At the Presbyterian College and Seminary in the port city of Kobe, a group of students gathered in a little group. "I can't believe Toyohiko is actually moving into the Shinkawa slums," said Takeshi. "That place is crawling with filth and crime. He's crazy!"

Hedeki chimed in. "He may be crazy, but have you heard him preach? The people swarm about him like flies when he gets out on the corners and alleys in Shinkawa. He says they do not really hear his message because he is living in comfort on this side of the bridge."

"Do you think that his year-long recovery in that remote fishing village put him off balance?" asked Jiro. "After all, he was near death with TB."

"No, that's not it," answered Takeshi. "Toyohiko believes Jesus' words literally. He says he must live with the people in order to understand and help them."

"I'm not sure anything can help the scum of Shinkawa," said Jiro with scorn. "There are more than ten thousand people living in that ten-block area, and half the children die of malnutrition before they're even five."

Hedeki looked thoughtful. "I admire Toyohiko," he said, "but it's not for me."

The seminary students watched as Toyohiko Kagawa with the help of an ex-convict pulled and pushed a creaking cart, loaded with Kagawa's few belongings, toward Shinkawa. The young men shook their heads, then returned to their studies.

Once across the bridge, Kagawa and his helper knew they were in the slums. A dreadful stench arose from open sewers, human waste, rotting garbage, and layers of filth. Flies buzzed, rats scavenged the refuse, and bedbugs crawled over dirty bedrolls. Disease was epidemic.

As the cart creaked over the cobblestones, the two movers heard noisy arguments as people fought, quarreled, and gambled. Ragged children, covered with sores, cried from hunger and abuse. Drunks staggered in the streets, derelicts slouched against the walls, prostitutes plied their trade, and suspicious eyes followed the cart.

"Aren't you afraid to live here?" asked Kagawa's helper. "You know a ghost lives in your shack. Belongs to the murdered renter before you. Why else do you think you got the place so cheap?"

"I am not afraid," replied Kagawa. He bought some straw mats for the floor of his six-foot-square bamboo-walled shack. But his stomach turned queasy when he saw the place. Dog excrement and crawling vermin covered the floors. Toyohiko cleaned until bedtime so he could move in. Because he had no money for lamp oil, he sat in the dark and prayed for courage. The people of Shinkawa had so many needs—for jobs with decent pay and safe working conditions, schools, medical care, and food centers. Toyohiko knew that bread alone wouldn't sustain them; he wanted them to know Christ.

As Kagawa tried to fall asleep to the din of slum life, anxious thoughts crowded his mind. Then a memory returned to strengthen his resolve. The scene was a hospital bed. He lay near death from tuberculosis, burning with fever. He had no pulse, and the doctor had

already signed the death certificate for his cremation. Suddenly God
became closer than a parent, inside him, all around him. His room
seemed transformed into a paradise and his quilt into a cloth of pure
gold. Joy filled him as he felt immersed in and united with God. His
fever disappeared, his pulse returned, and he recovered.[4] Remembering
that now gave him courage to face his new challenge.

From the beginning of his stay in Shinkawa, Kagawa was besieged
with requests for food, money, and a place to stay. First a frightful-
looking beggar covered with a skin disease asked to move in. Toyohiko
cherished his privacy, but he felt he must demonstrate Christ's love, not
just talk about it. He invited the man to stay.

Next came a bedraggled bean-curd vendor who begged for lodging. "A drunk knocked over my wicker baskets and all my bean-curd
spilled in the street," he wailed. "I was so mad I hit him on the head.
But I didn't mean to kill him. Now his ghost keeps following me."
Kagawa took the vendor in and often held his hand at night to calm
his fears of being chased by the murdered man.

Others moved in, some for long term, some for a few days, alcoholics, syphilitic beggars, men and women scourged by disease. On
his small seminary scholarship, twenty-one-year-old Toyohiko supported his unconventional family by taking an extra job sweeping chim-
neys. Often there was only watered-down rice gruel for all of them
to eat.

At one time ten people were sharing Kagawa's small quarters, so
he finally had to remove a wall to make room for the crowd. One person
was dying of tuberculosis; others had skin diseases. Kagawa shared his
sleeping mat and coverlet with a man who had trachoma and caught
the eye disease, which nearly blinded him.

Kagawa was an enigma to the Shinkawa residents, but soon their
curiosity turned to trust and they began to take his preaching to heart.
Others, however, took advantage of his idealism. They pulled knives
on him, demanded money, fired shots into his home, smashed his dishes,
stole his cooking pots, and threw rocks at him. A drunk knocked out
four front teeth. A brothel owner threatened him with a pistol because
Toyohiko preached against prostitution. Beggars got the clothes off his
back because he couldn't refuse those who asked. In all his encounters,
Kagawa tried to imitate the life of Jesus. When a smile couldn't solve
his problems with violent troublemakers, he ran away.

As the people flocked to Kagawa for advice and help, he saw the
need for love in action. He added a room to his shack and turned it
into a dispensary. He started a Sunday school, made house calls on the

Shinkawa residents, cleaned their filthy hovels, washed their bedsores, secured their medicine, and arranged for doctor appointments. Wherever he went, he listened as men, women, and children poured out their fears, angers, and frustrations.

After about a year, Kagawa obtained funding from sympathetic sources so he could expand his work among the Shinkawa residents. He rented apartments next door and knocked down the walls to create a chapel, study, and rooms for meetings and classes. Eventually he established a free health clinic which was funded with proceeds from *Across the Death-Line*, his novel based on the slums.

Toyohiko was fortunate to meet and marry a woman who shared his vision. Right after the marriage ceremony, he and Haru "honeymooned" in their hut in Shinkawa which they shared with destitute people.

In spite of all the demands on his life, Kagawa always took time to pray and meditate. He arose before dawn for his quiet time, then went out on the streets to preach before beginning his hectic schedule. In the evening he was back on the street corners, preaching. After his ordination in 1917, he chose to continue living and working in Shinkawa.

Kagawa soon realized that the problems of the slums were so enormous that preaching alone was ineffective. Massive changes in society itself were necessary, so he also began pleading the cause of the laborers to management and officials. When the workers called on him to lead them, he promised to do so only if they refrained from violence. He began ambitious programs of reform in which he started labor unions, a labor college, and opened consumers' cooperatives where people could buy food and clothing at low prices. He constantly preached Christ's peaceful way to settle disputes. He was imprisoned a number of times for his activities on behalf of laborers.

Kagawa also started milk depots and clinics for children and was active in suffrage campaigns for both men and women. After the great 1923 earthquake in Japan, the government asked him to serve on various commissions in the capital of Tokyo and head up relief and reconstruction work.

Kagawa was joined by other reformers as he spoke and wrote constantly about the evils of slum life. This resulted in new laws that gradually put an end to slums and created decent living conditions for victims of the quake as well.

As Kagawa became recognized worldwide, he was invited to speak in countries all over the world. By this time he was earning quite a bit from the sale of his books, but he gave most of it away or spent it on projects for the needy. He believed that the church and its people must not be content with merely saying beautiful things. They must not remove themselves from the dirty business of life's problems if they were to follow Jesus' example.

Kagawa reproached Christians who were more concerned with maintaining their buildings and preaching conversion to the poor, while they, themselves, lived in comfort and debated doctrines. He said that believers often "talked mightily of doctrine on Sunday but ignored the poor at the church steps."[5]

"All the idols and the temples and cathedrals are nothing but symbols," he said. "All forms and ceremonies are but supplements. Jesus Christ is the greatest educator in the world—a teacher of love."[6]

Kagawa could in no way reconcile Jesus' lack of resistance with military action of any kind. He was imprisoned for speaking out against Japan's involvement in various wars. "To be real Christians we must belong to Heaven first, then to our nation. I belong to God first, then to Japan; therefore everywhere I feel at home. You may think that your country belongs to you, but it belongs to God first."[7]

As events moved closer to World War II and the war hysteria heightened, Kagawa continued his uncompromising pacifism. Because he insisted that loyalty to Christ was higher than loyalty to the state or emperor, he was followed by the secret police. They monitored all his activities, attended his services, and took notes on what he said; then they reported to headquarters. Time and again Kagawa was arrested, and placards around the city proclaimed, KAGAWA IS A TRAITOR TO JAPAN! DEATH TO KAGAWA! His once popular books were banned and many of them publicly burned.

Kagawa gave hundreds of speeches in the United States and Japan, pleading for peace and criticizing militarism in both countries. This put him out of step with both the East and the West.

After the defeat of Japan, those who had scoffed at his ideas during the war then called him to positions of leadership. Prince Higashi-Kuni told him, "We need a new standard of ethics in our country like that of Jesus Christ. Buddhism can never teach us to forgive our enemies; nor can Shintoism. Only Jesus Christ was able to love his enemies."[8]

Even Emperor Hirohito called Kagawa into his presence because he wanted to hear more of the Christian way. After a long session with the emperor, Kagawa drew his tattered Bible from his robe and read, "Whoever would be great among you must be your servant."[9] Then

Kagawa added, "Only through service can a person or a nation be great."[10]

Eventually people all over the world recognized Dr. Kagawa for his courage, humanity, and Christian witness. Although times of retreat and reflection were an important part of Kagawa's life, he insisted that, "Mountain retreats and religious systems can never constitute a Gospel. True salvation begins with the heart. If salvation is not realised in the crowd, and in the bustling city, a true living religion has not yet begun its work."[11]

Notes

1. Cyril J. Davey, *Kagawa of Japan* (New York: Abingdon Press, 1960), 25.

2. Robert Schildgen, *Toyohiko Kagawa: Apostle of Love and Social Justice* (Berkeley: Centenary Books, 1988), 19.

3. Davey, *Japan*, 18.

4. Schildgen, *Apostle*, 36.

5. Ibid., 16.

6. Davey, *Japan*, 88.

7. Ibid., 102.

8. Ibid., 125.

9. Ibid., 132.

10. H. J. Charter, *Kagawa* (Ceylon, India: Christian Literature Society, 1933), 30.

11. Ibid., 30.

4 *Jane Addams* 1860–1935

Jane was visiting Spain. She left the bullfight, disgusted with the whole affair. Five bulls and several horses killed! The crowd surged about her, laughing, chatting, and seemingly indifferent to the bloody spectacle behind them. Jane wondered what moral depravity gave people pleasure in watching humans and animals injured or killed.

Jane had seen society's extremes over the past few years. With her family wealth she had studied abroad and traveled extensively with friends. Back at her hotel, restless thoughts kept her from sleep. "I'm just lulling myself into indifference," she lectured herself. "All this study and travel. Spain, England, France, Germany . . . And where is it getting me?"

Jane thought of all the intellectual pursuits in which people were engaged, herself included. "But have these had any effect on the moral development of society?" she asked. "If so, I certainly haven't seen any evidence."

Her mind went back to childhood. She was two when her mother died, and her tall, Quaker father, respected by everyone for his integrity, had been a powerful influence on her life. She clearly remembered a particular Sunday morning in her eighth year. She had just dressed herself for Sunday school in a beautiful, new cloak. Admiring her image in the mirror, she imagined what the other little girls would say when they saw her new outfit. Proudly Jane went downstairs.

"Thee looks very fine, Jane," said her father. "That is surely a nice cloak. But it is so much prettier than anything the other little girls will be wearing, that I think thee should not wear it. Thy old cloak will keep thee warm enough, and then thee won't make any of the other little girls at church feel bad."[1]

The incident reminded her of a question that had continued to plague her all during her growing years. "Why are there so many inequities in the world?" Her family enjoyed spacious living in the pleasant country, but many people lacked even the basic necessities. She would always remember the time she had accompanied her father on a business trip to a mill town not far away. She had been shocked by the squalor of the neighborhood, the filthy streets stinking with garbage, ragged people living in rotting tenements, and shacks with broken windows. "Some day when I grow up," Jane had told her father, "I'm going to have a great big house. But it won't be among other big houses. It will stand right in the middle of horrid little houses like these, and I will help the people who live all around."[2]

Now, traveling as she was, Jane saw the needy masses everywhere. The last time she came abroad she toured Mile End Road in London's East End with a missionary group. It was late on a Saturday night. From the top section of the omnibus, she had a good view of the slum area that teemed with activity as people of all ages struggled to survive in a jungle of filth, poverty, and disease.

Vendors were hauling in wagonloads of overripe and rotting fruits and vegetables to auction off cheaply. Because Sunday laws decreed that no produce could be sold on the Sabbath, whatever wouldn't keep until Monday was sold in poverty areas on Saturday night.

The crowds swarmed around a produce wagon. The light from gas jets flickered on the hard, shrewd faces of people who were daily forced to live by their wits. A vendor held a rotting cabbage high. "What am I bid for this here fine head?" he shouted. A scraggly man bid a penny, and the vendor flung the spoiled cabbage to his filthy, outstretched hands. The receiver dropped to the curb and tore savagely into the wormy vegetable. Within a few minutes, he devoured the entire thing.

The memory of the slum scene dimmed. "How can I live in comfort and do nothing when I see so many people living in misery?" Jane asked herself. "It's time for action."

Jane had felt the same need for action when she was baptized into the Presbyterian church as a new member. She believed that the church was important to the community and one ought to belong, because belonging was an outward symbol that confirmed what one felt within. In this new fellowship she hoped to find a spirit of unity that brought people together in spite of their differences in personality, race, or culture.

As Jane tossed on her bed, she began to reminisce about the concerts and social gatherings she had attended on this trip and the many privileged young people she had met. She noted how they were sheltered and guarded from every disappointment by doting parents . . . "simply smothered and sickened with advantages. It is like eating a sweet dessert the first thing in the morning," she said.[3] "And if I'm not careful, I'll fall into the trap of believing that all the art exhibits, concerts, travel, and study are a preparation for great things to come, when in reality they might be just a defense for idleness."[4]

As Jane pondered these thoughts, familiar lines from somewhere kept coming back. "Weary of myself and sick of asking, what I am and what I want to be."[5]

Her floundering wearied her, and the bullfight jolted her into seeing that she needed goals for her life. An idea that had been forming in the back of her mind ever since childhood surfaced again. Perhaps she could live among the poor in Chicago and develop programs for them. The next day Jane shared her idea with her companions and talked about it frequently as they continued their sightseeing through Spain and northern France.

Some months later Jane attended a world mission conference in London. She was surprised and delighted to discover mission programs being carried out in the city in which cultural advantages were made available to the poor. Jane was impressed with the sincere tone of the programs without the condescending manner typical of so much mission activity.

Jane's desire to be of service finally crystallized into a decision. She would open a settlement house in the Chicago slums. This would be a place where communication between the classes could be restored and where poor people would feel welcome and among friends. She would also have a chance to share culture and beauty with them and enrich their drab lives.

Ellen Gates Starr vowed to help. After returning to the U.S., the two young women searched the Chicago neighborhoods until they found an enormous, old house with spacious rooms, large halls, fireplaces, and piazzas. The house had been built by Mr. Charles Hull thirty-three years earlier. Most of the rooms were presently vacant, although some were under lease and others used for factory storage.

The house was set in the midst of crumbling tenements in a neighborhood of Jewish, Italian, Russian, Polish, Bohemian, Canadian, Irish, Chinese, German, and other immigrants.

This community had many needs. The tenements were without running water, toilets, or bathtubs, and few had fire escapes. Landlords had no incentive to spend money on improvements and reduce the income they were making on these squalid dwellings. The horse stables were also in foul condition, and streets and alleys were narrow, crowded, and poorly lit. Overflowing garbage attracted flies, rats, and disease.

This was just the place for a settlement. Jane rented the empty rooms of the big house, and Mr. Hull's niece promised that soon the whole place would be available to her.

With help, Jane and Ellen fixed up their new house and filled it with lovely furnishings from many places. They wanted this to be a place where they did things *with* people, not just *for* them. They also hoped to bring an appreciation of beauty and art to the impoverished people who came there from their own drab surroundings. They called it the Hull-House.

The neighbors were quite suspicious in the beginning. "Why are these well-to-do women renting a house in *our* neighborhood when they can live anywhere they wish?" someone asked.

A man shook his head. "Yah, it's the strangest thing I've ever met in my experience."

"But you know what?" added a third, "I saw them down on their hands and knees this morning, doing their own scrubbing and fixing."

To Jane and Ellen it did not seem strange. It seemed natural to feed the hungry, care for the sick, bring joy to the young, and comfort to the aged.

As soon as the house was ready, Jane started programs to help the people in the neighborhood. She started activities to keep young girls off the streets after long boring hours in the factory. She organized a nursery, a kindergarten, classes in woodworking, basketry, handwork, sewing, cooking, and music instruction. Reading clubs gave young and old an opportunity to read stories from many countries and other good literature.

Cleanliness was also a luxury for many of the tenement dwellers. Mothers, worn out from long hours at the factory, didn't feel like hauling water from an outdoor, communal faucet up several flights of stairs in order to keep their families clean. To relieve this problem three public bathtubs were installed in the basement of Hull-House. The tubs were so popular that Miss Addams persuaded the Chicago Board of Health to install a public bath. Grudgingly they complied. "No one will use them," they complained. The facility was such a success, however, that more were built around the city.

A gym was later added onto Hull-House for swimming, basketball, and dancing. Lively evening and social clubs mixed up the nationalities and helped them overcome some of their suspicions about each other. One woman admitted losing her prejudice against the Italians through such activities. "I'm ashamed of the way I used to call them all 'dagos,' " she said, "and now I see that they are quite like other people."

Young, black-eyed Angelina summed it all up after her hard day in the factory. "We have swell times in our Hull-House club. Our floor in the gym puts it all over the old dancehalls for a jolly good hop . . . no saloon next door with all that crowd, good classy music, and the right sort of girls and fellows. Then sometimes our club has a real party in the coffee-house. That's what I call a fine, cozy time; makes a girl glad she's living."[6]

Day nurseries were also a priority because many little children were unattended while their parents worked in the factories. Before the day nurseries there were some unfortunate incidents. One child fell out a third-story window, another developed a curved spine from being tied to the leg of a kitchen table all day for three years. On hot, stifling summer days the little ones were often put out on the street. At Hull-House mothers learned the elements of child care and shared their problems of child-rearing.

Because children as young as four sometimes worked in the factories, Jane and others belonging to the Hull-House community worked on getting laws passed against child labor. They wanted school attendance to be required, the employment age for children raised to sixteen, and inspections of the workplace in order to see that health and safety regulations were followed. One day two spokespersons for the factory owners took Jane to lunch and offered her $50,000 if she would drop the "radical nonsense" about the sweatshop bill. They said, "With this money, Hull-House can become the largest institution on the West Side of Chicago."

"It is not my ambition to become the largest institution on the West Side," Jane replied. "Our concern is to protect our neighbors from poor working conditions. If destroying Hull-House can do this, then we will cheerfully destroy Hull-House and sing a *Te Deum* on its ruins."[7] In 1903 the child-labor bill became law in Illinois.

One day a woman named Mrs. Morgan rushed into Hull-House, soaking wet. "My husband is in prison," she sobbed, "and my family doesn't have food." She was returning from the county agent's office carrying paper bags filled with beans and flour. On the way home it began to rain. Mrs. Morgan was worried about her bags so she boarded a street car, but the rain-soaked bags burst all over the car.

"Slob," yelled the conductor, "look at the mess you've made! And where's your fare?" Mrs. Morgan tried to tell him what had happened, but he was too angry to listen. He put her off near Hull-House, and when she unloaded her problems to Jane, Mrs. Morgan did not curse her husband, the conductor, or the rain, but poverty itself. Besides providing a sympathetic ear, Miss Addams arranged to replace the food that was lost. At Hull-House Mrs. Morgan also discovered opportunities to attend classes in cooking and child care, and to enjoy socializing.

Another enormous problem was the high incidence of disease resulting from constantly overflowing garbage boxes. For four years Jane complained to City Hall, but the situation did not improve. Finally, Jane and the Hull-House Women's Club took action and tramped the blocks and alleys on hot summer evenings to inspect the streets and alleys of the nineteenth ward. They reported 1,037 garbage violations! When Jane applied for the job of garbage collector herself, the mayor appointed her to be a garbage inspector, the only paid job she ever held.

Jane was up every morning by 6:00 to follow the garbage collectors on their rounds and see that they picked up *all* the garbage. "There are two dead horses you've neglected to pick up," she told one collector.

"No room in my cart," he complained.

"Then you'll just have to make more trips to the dump," Jane insisted. "Those carcasses carry disease."

The collector grumbled, so Jane went to see the contractor. "We need more wagons to pick up the garbage," she told him.

"Aw, Miss, I can't afford no more wagons."

"You're more concerned with profit than the health and lives of the people you are supposed to serve," she told him. After much arguing, the contractor gave in and increased the number of wagons for the Hull-House ward, complaining all the while that he would end up in the poorhouse.

One rainy day there was a frantic knock on the door of Hull-House. "Come quick," the visitor said. Jane grabbed her umbrella and followed the messenger to the home of an elderly German immigrant. The woman was hugging a chest of drawers while the workmen tried to pry her loose so they could move her out. Her eyes were wild and she made squealing noises like a trapped animal in distress.

"They're taking her to the poorhouse," the neighbors volunteered. "She's only got crusts of bread to eat and no money."

Jane quickly figured out that all the woman's treasured possessions were in that chest.

"Go back to your office and tell them that Hull-House will take care of the woman's food and rent," Jane told the men. The neighbors promised to help too.

Relieved of their unpleasant task, the men left. With relief the woman collapsed into a chair, exhausted, but smiling.

Another woman rushed to Hull-House sobbing. "The landlord wants to throw us out. Grandmother is bedridden and she is picking the plaster off the walls and making holes in it. We all have to work in the factory and now we have no place to go."

That afternoon a Hull-House worker brought the grandmother a basket of rainbow-colored paper, paste, and scissors. She showed the woman how to make brightly colored chains to decorate her room, then promised to return and mend the wall. The next day the old grandmother's eyes sparkled as she showed off the chains she had made. When the landlord saw the mended wall and decorative chains he agreed to let the family stay. Hull-House kept the old woman's hands busy to the end of her days.

Motivated by the message of the gospel, Jane Addams worked all her life to better the lives of poor and vulnerable people. More than two thousand people streamed through Hull-House weekly, participating in its many programs. Jane Addams was an articulate, knowledgeable fighter. She struggled to bring about many laws: the eight-hour work day, safer practices in industry, minimum wages, sickness and unemployment insurance, and the vote for women. She organized many activities for the cause of peace and justice. She believed that it was easy enough for comfortable Christians to have ideas about the poor, but to express the true spirit of Christ, they must see Christ in each person and put their words into action.

Notes

1.   Jane Addams, *Twenty Years at Hull-House* (New York: The Macmillan Company, 1939), 13–14.

2.   Ibid., 3, 5.

3.   Ibid., 73.

4. Ibid., 86.

5. Ibid., 78.

6. Mary R. Parkman, *Heroines of Service* (New York: Century, 1917), 314-15.

7. Addams, *Twenty Years,* 33–34.

5 *Paul-Émile Léger* 1904–91

It was Christmas Eve, 1923. Midnight Mass was over, and the church had emptied. Young Paul-Émile felt despair as he slipped into a corner of the choir loft to meditate and pray for guidance. Would this respiratory illness that was ruining his life never go away? Already it had forced him to drop out of school and give up his plans to seek an academic career. What kind of goals were realistic for him now? What did God want him to do with his life anyway?

As Paul-Émile sat in the quiet sanctuary, his thoughts went back over the highs and lows of his past nineteen years. A great joy of his childhood had been to serve as an altar boy at St. Anicet in Montréal where he grew up. He remembered how he loved to read and to preach sermons from the organ stool while he pretended to officiate at the Mass. Another favorite pastime was giving political speeches in front of the mirror.

His gentle grandmother looked after him and later on his brother, nine years younger, while his mother and father ran the village store. From his grandmother Paul-Émile learned to revere a God of mystery, love, and beauty. She taught him to pray and told him stories about Jesus and the saints who cared for the hungry and helpless.

Looking back, Paul-Émile appreciated the stability and tenderness of his home life. His parents were loving, yet strict. Like his grandmother, they taught him to choose what was right and to be sensitive to the "breath of the Holy Spirit."

At age twelve the local priest persuaded Paul-Émile's parents to send him to the junior seminary at Sainte Thérèse. He loved scholarly pursuits! He excelled in oratory and in all his subjects, but poor health prevented him from continuing his studies. When he moved with his family from Québec to Lancaster, Ontario, he was lonely in his new surroundings and ill as well. He tried working in the family store where he had a future opportunity to take over the business. He also tried working as a mechanic, butcher, and electrician, but none of these jobs suited him.

As Paul-Émile reminisced, he agonized over his future. In the quiet sanctuary he prayed, "How can I serve you, God? What direction should my life take?" His heart pleaded for an answer.

Out of nowhere, he heard a voice, clear and distinct. "You will become a priest!"[1] Paul-Émile was startled. Was this his imagination? No! He knew it wasn't. What he heard was an actual voice!

Joy filled the young man as he realized that God had spoken to him. God had a plan for his life after all! "From the instant I heard the sentence," Paul-Émile said later, "I knew that my road was forever marked out and that nothing could prevent me from fulfilling my dream. Not even illness."[2] From then on, Paul-Émile gave little thought to his health, but vigorously pursued his goal.

Forty-six years later, Paul-Émile had reached the pinnacle of his career. His years in the priesthood had been rich and full, and included serving as Archbishop of Montréal. Three years after that appointment he was elevated to the position of cardinal at age forty-nine, and was one of the youngest archbishops ever to receive this honor. At sixty-three Cardinal Léger had power, position, influence, recognition, and a string of achievements, honors, medals, awards, and conferments that were acknowledged worldwide.

Yet there were times when Cardinal Léger felt weighed down by church bureaucracy, ecclesiastical minutiae, squabbles to settle, organizations to oversee, and documents to sign. He was in constant demand to bless new structures, lend his influence to new undertakings, and participate in ceremonies. As he thought of all the pomp and ritual that accompanied his office, he wondered, "How much of this helps relieve the suffering of the world?" He believed "the continuing use of splendour is an obstacle to working for the poor in the spirit of the gospel."[3] All through his life social concerns had been a priority, and throughout his career he had carried out ambitious programs to help the young and old, the poor, sick, and homeless.

One night the Cardinal tossed in his bed, unable to sleep. Finally he turned on his light and began to leaf through a magazine depicting the suffering lepers of Africa. The photos reminded him of his visit to Africa four years earlier. He had been shocked by the appalling living conditions in the leper colonies, and on his return to Canada, he established a movement called *Fame Pereo*, Latin for "I am dying of hunger." This organization eventually provided aid to more than eighty leprosariums in twenty African countries, including rehabilitation houses, dispensaries, schools, residences, research centers, and scientific equipment. Yet this was not enough for the Cardinal.

"What more can I do for Africa?" he asked, studying his magazine. Just then he noticed a little plea at the bottom of one page. "We ask alms for lepers dying of hunger." The Cardinal was struck by the horror of the situation. Not only were these people struggling with the debilitating disease of leprosy, but they were starving to death besides.

He thought of the indifference North Americans and Europeans showed to the poverty of the Third World. He preached repeatedly about the disparity between rich and poor nations, and the "collective sin that the well-fed commit in complete disregard of justice and humanity,"[4] but his words seemed to fall on deaf ears. People continued their relentless pursuit of materialism and self-indulgence.

Cardinal Léger began to wonder: What if I were to go back to Africa to help these people and become a simple, parish priest again? Finally he made a decision: "I feel the time has come when God is asking me for deeds, not merely words. If I make the right decision, perhaps then the people who haven't understood what I have been saying, will understand what I am doing."[5] He remembered the words his mother had written him when he became a Cardinal. "From the time you were a very small child, you gave your life to Jesus."[6] That love for Jesus had shaped his life and now was driving him toward a new purpose. Finally he slept.

The next day the sun shone brightly as the Cardinal went about his work, but his nighttime resolve never dimmed. He conferred with Pope Paul VI as he moved toward his final decision.

On Thursday, November 9, 1967, Cardinal Léger presented a formal statement to the press. He explained that after receiving permission from the Holy See, he was resigning his position as Cardinal of the Montréal Archdiocese and was going to Africa as a simple parish priest. "Faith is before everything else the witness of a life,"[7] he said.

"The time has come to go from words to actions. I wish to dedicate the few years allotted to me to giving spiritual and material assistance to the lepers, and so I am leaving for Africa."[8]

People were stunned by Cardinal Léger's announcement. A cardinal giving up all the honor of his position for lepers? As he prepared for his journey, someone asked him, "Don't you think there are enough problems right here in Montréal to deal with, and by going to Africa aren't you escaping from them?"

Cardinal Léger answered, "You have all the means necessary to give these people what they want here, because you live in an affluent society and civilization. When you think that 200 million Africans have an average salary of $50 a year, I think that I can go with easiness."[9]

On December 11 the Cardinal tearfully waved good-bye to his friends and country and departed for Africa. When he arrived in Cameroon he was greeted by Archbishop Jean Zoa of Yaoundé to whom he had offered his services. Curious crowds gathered round to see the famous man who had chosen to live among them! He had a warm smile for everyone as he shook their hands and withered stumps, patted the children, and kissed the babies who played with his pectoral cross.

The Cardinal found the needs in Cameroon staggering. Besides basic physical necessities, medical needs were enormous. He spent his beginning months working in the leprosarium while also offering Mass, comforting lonely hearts, praying with the sick, helping troubled families, and rising in the middle of the night to be with those facing death. Archbishop Zoa commented that the sixty-three-year-old cardinal had the energy of a man of forty.

Cardinal Léger amazed the Africans as he listened sensitively to their opinions and ideas. Most foreigners rarely listened, but instead tried to impose their own agendas on the people.

The Cardinal soon discovered that organizations helping the lepers were working effectively, so he gave much thought about where he could be the most use in Cameroon. His answer came by working closely with Archbishop Zoa and the Cameroonian medical authorities. Together they decided that the most neglected people of Cameroon were the handicapped. Polio crippled thousands of children every year. They dragged themselves through the dust, unable to walk, and no effort was made to treat them or train them to become independent. Cardinal Léger with these African experts decided that the best plan was to build a rehabilitation center.

First the Cardinal got the support of every chief in neighboring villages. The Cameroonian government donated beautiful land on a hill overlooking Yaoundé and the Canadians raised money for an initial investment. The goal would be to help children learn to walk and become self-sufficient, and to train the Cameroonians so they could eventually take over the center.

Cardinal Léger moved into a simple trailer home alongside the construction site so he could oversee the work and be sure that incoming funds were properly channeled. By his presence he was also able to settle inevitable disputes. While the center was being built, the Cardinal also established "Cardinal Léger and his Endeavours" to raise money for developing nations and to fund the projects he had already begun. In time the endeavors included ambitious projects in health, education, and agriculture in Third World countries. "I will not live forever," he reminded his friends, so his goal was to establish enterprises that would continue long after he was gone.

By 1972 the rehabilitation center was ready for use. It consisted of more than a dozen buildings, including classrooms, dormitories, rooms for physiotherapy and occupational therapy, prosthetics workshops, a chapel, and gardens.

Although the Cardinal was always on the move, he sometimes spent a day at the new center. Such a day might have gone like this:

Early in the morning, the Cardinal welcomes commuters who arrive at the dispensary by bus or on foot. Here patients receive treatment or counseling for their health problems. The rest of the center serves mainly children, many of whom stay round the clock.

Cardinal Léger strolls into a classroom where a handicapped African instructor, Oscar Njanga, is explaining math problems on the blackboard. Mr. Njanga tries to keep the children comfortable and the classroom atmosphere relaxed. Walls display maps, posters, and lively artwork. Eager children listen to their teacher from wheelchairs or from rolling carts as they lie on their stomachs. The Cardinal helps a boy with his math. The children work hard and Mr. Njanga is pleased with their progress. To reward them, he takes out his guitar and the class joins in the music by clapping out rhythms. The Cardinal claps too.

In the hall Cardinal Léger meets little Valentin, nearly lost in a big wheelchair. His mother is bringing him for an extended stay, and Valentin is in tears because he is afraid of the unfamiliar surroundings. The gentle Cardinal introduces him to children who are playing a game. Before long Valentin smiles and joins in.

Cardinal Léger next visits the prosthetics shop where skilled workers—many of whom are Africans who live with physical handicaps—are measuring, cutting, and sewing orthopedic shoes and fashioning braces and limbs. Some are carving crutches from the cheap and abundant mahogany of the area. The workers are pleased to show the Cardinal the devices they have created.

Paul-Émile moves on to occupational therapy where doctors, nurses, and physiotherapists from all over the world are at work. A mother is learning how to massage the limbs and paralyzed muscles of her little boy so she can continue treatment when the child is home again. Further on, boys and girls are learning to sew, weave, make baskets, and draw or paint pictures. A little girl whose hair has many tiny braids is pleased with the colors she has mixed on her paper. The Cardinal compliments her on her creation.

In another area a little girl with frightened eyes lies on a cart while her legs are fitted with braces. Big tears roll down her cheeks. The Cardinal lovingly comforts her, then helps her stand for the first time. He guides her to take a faltering step. She smiles. Then another step. Her smile grows bigger. "I can walk! I can walk!" she squeals. Eighty-five percent of the children at the center learn to walk.

On the grounds Cardinal Léger finds boys and girls with braces and crutches learning to push carts, kick balls, and wheel around in walkers. A grinning nine-year-old in his walker shouts, "Look out! Here I come!"

While Cardinal Léger is on the grounds, Chief Jean Essomba is brought by car for his daily therapy. He is dressed in brightly colored clothes with a large rooster design on the front. His legs are in braces too, but with his crutches he walks up to the Cardinal, smiling broadly. The chief had polio in infancy and now at fifty-eight, he is learning to walk for the first time. Faithfully each day he does his exercises.

The center includes children of all races and religions. "I believe that what we must bring the people here is not complicated theology," says Cardinal Léger, "but the witness of a life consecrated to God. Such a life is not a series of extraordinary events, but simply loving attention to the needs of others."[10]

Throughout his years in Africa, Cardinal Léger kept up a very intense pace. His accomplishments to help suffering humanity were enormous. "The gap separating rich countries and poor countries widens and deepens more and more each day," he said. "The time has come for the cry for justice to penetrate the conscience of rich countries."[11]

At age seventy-five Cardinal Léger was ready to return home, but first he turned control of the rehabilitation center over to the Cameroonians. After arriving in Montréal, a journalist asked him if he was going to retire. "I will rest only from the day all the poor will have a little bread and a little water on their tables," the Cardinal answered.[12]

The Cardinal continued a full schedule until he died on November 13, 1991, at age eighty-seven. As he had hoped, the charitable works in his memory continue on all over the world. Certainly his life modeled his words, "I strive only to make the gospel not seem a lie."[13]

The list of Cardinal Léger's accomplishments is impressive, and it seems important to list a few of these: A progressive leader in the Roman Catholic church, Paul-Émile Léger founded a seminary in Japan before World War II, served as rector of the Canadian College in Rome after World War II, organized an extensive network of charity drives to help Pope Pius XII secure aid for war victims, served as a conciliatory leader in Québec's Quiet Revolution, was an influential mover in the Vatican II Council, and was involved in the "Jules and Paul-Émile Léger Foundation," an organization that was created by a special law of the Canadian Parliament to support all the Cardinal's endeavors at home and in nearly a hundred countries. (Jules Léger, a brother of Paul-Émile, was an internationally known Canadian statesman and also a champion of the poor.) After returning from Africa, Cardinal Léger took on positions of leadership to help Asian refugees and was influential in hundreds of new projects to provide aid in many countries. At home he visited prisons and participated in thousands of forums to encourage help for the poorest of the world.

Notes

1. *Share . . . Special Edition* (Outremont, Québec: Jules and Paul-Émile Léger Foundation, 1992), 6.
2. Ibid., 6.
3. James Duggan, *Paul-Émile Léger* (Don Mills: Fitzhenry and Whiteside, 1981), 45.
4. Ibid., 48.
5. "A Life with Lustre," Toronto *Telegram,* Saturday, 2 Dec. 1967.
6. Chantal Théorêt, ed., *In Remembrance . . . 1904–1991, Cardinal Paul-Émile Léger* (Outremont, Québec: Partnership Publishing, 1992), 18.
7. "A Good Man's Great Decision," Toronto *Star Weekly Magazine,* 9 Dec. 1967, p. 21.
8. Ibid., 23.
9. "Crisis of Faith," Edmonton *Western Catholic Reporter,* 16 Nov. 1967, p. 9.
10. Ken Bell and Henriette Major, *A Man and His Mission, Cardinal Léger in Africa* (Scarborough, Ontario: Prentice-Hall, 1976), 70.
11. *Share . . . Special Edition,* 25.
12. Ibid., 4.
13. Duggan, *Léger,* 59.

6 *Marie Sandvik* 1902–92

It was 1940, and Marie was scouting the drab and dirty Gateway area of Skid Row in Minneapolis. Drunks shuffled along the spit-covered sidewalks, and unwashed derelicts, prostitutes, and ragged panhandlers milled about the foul-smelling streets. Some begged for a dime as the young woman passed or made obscene remarks. But Marie ignored their advances as she surveyed each building and bar, each broken-down storefront. Could she find what she was looking for?

Finally she saw a place, Angelo's Bar on Washington and Nicollet Avenues. A sign read, "For Rent. See Christ upstairs." (The sign-maker had tried to abbreviate Chris Christianson.)

Marie took all her savings, rented the bar, and moved into the room behind it, along with rats, cockroaches, bedbugs, and lice from the tenement above. As she tried to sleep that night with the city din in her ears, she remembered well her own struggle to earn a living more than twenty years ago. She had not forgotten the gnawing hunger pains, tattered clothes, and the awful feeling that no one cared. She had vowed then that someday she would return to the streets, open a mission, and fulfill her dream to bring help and hope to people like the ones she had seen today.

Her thoughts drifted far away to Norway, her childhood homeland. The memories were so clear in her mind. From the time she was little, she loved to preach, to the sheep . . . to herself . . . or to anyone who would listen.

She loved books and learning and memorized Luther's catechism, whole chapters from the Bible, and literature from the great poets and writers. Because she was always talking and reciting to herself, some people called her "the crazy kid."

One day a well-known Lutheran preacher visited her town. When Marie told him that she wanted to live her life for the Lord, he was impressed. He placed his hands on her head and asked God to bless her and use her to do his will. He smiled and said, "This little girl is going to move mountains." Marie thought of *Helvetesberget* (or "Hell's Mountain") near her home. Little did she know then that in the future she would struggle to remove mountains of drunkenness, drug addiction, prostitution, abuse, hunger, want, and crime.

Marie came to America at age seventeen because as a poor orphan, her chances of getting an education in Norway were slim. She worked her way through high school in Minneapolis, selling Bibles and Christian magazines. Many days she made so little money that she went hungry.

Soon after her arrival she sobbed into her pillow, "Dear God, what will become of me? I thought money grew on trees in America." She was famished and ragged and her shoes were worn out. But Marie reminded herself that she belonged to God, so she would make it!

In college she washed pots and pans for a restaurant and edited a Norwegian magazine, *Nordvesten*. After graduating with honors from both high school and college, Marie attended a Congregational seminary in Seattle because at that time the Lutheran seminaries did not accept female students. Later she worked as a children's evangelist and also set up camps to feed hungry children. And now she had returned to these dangerous streets alone, yet not alone.

Early the next morning Marie awoke to sunshine. As she looked over her empty bank account she thought of Philippians 4:19, "My God will supply every need of yours." With this promise she would open her mission.

First she needed a piano. She visited several music stores but quickly learned that depending on God to supply all her needs was not the kind of credit rating that the business world understood. At one music store she began to tell the salesman that God had called her to open a church in the slums, but he eyed her suspiciously. Fortunately the manager overheard the conversation. He hurried toward Marie, smiling. "A church in the slums, eh? And you have a real Norwegian accent. Most of the poor people in the Gateway are Scandinavians who have forgotten their childhood training."

With tears he recited the words to the first hymn he had learned as a child in Norway, "O Hail the Day When the Saved Shall Assemble." Then he promised Marie a piano and said she could pay for it as she was able. He added, "I think that wonderful old hymn of ours will see you through."

Next Marie needed chairs. She went to a furniture store and found just the type of chair she wanted. She didn't have the courage to tell the Jewish proprietor that her only bank account was the promise from Philippians 4:19 that God would supply all her needs. Nevertheless, he generously offered her 150 folding chairs that very afternoon to tide her over until the ones she ordered would arrive.

That evening, an unfamiliar woman's voice with a Norwegian accent spoke from what had once been Angelo's bar. "The Master is here and calleth for thee. I am offering you a new life to live, not a check to take to the tavern. You have tried everything. Why don't you try the Jesus of your childhood?"[1]

More than two hundred people off the street attended that first service. "I didn't speak to them of hell and damnation," said Marie. "No, no. I didn't want to scare them. I only wanted them to know I cared for them, loved them and wanted to help them."[2]

The first convert was an unemployed bartender with a Ph.D. who had once been an editor of a city newspaper. Now he was unkempt, and his dirty toes poked through threadbare stockings. He was sick of being powerless over his ugly existence. Marie's message touched his heart. Was new life in Christ for him? He staggered to the front, knelt at the altar, and prayed for help from God and for forgiveness. After that experience, he worked six years for Marie, growing in faith until his death.

Day after day people with hungry hearts flocked to the mission. They came by the hundreds—all kinds and all ages—yet they all had one thing in common, empty lives tyrannized by sin.

Soon church people of many denominations began reaching out to help Marie at her mission. With this new support, the work expanded. Weary drifters flocked to the former bar, grateful to be in a place where someone said they were important. After attending services, they were offered food and clothing. Marie rented three floors of the flophouse above the mission to provide a place for those with nowhere to go but the streets.

Her motto was, "We come with the gospel in one hand, and food in the other."[3] She said she didn't want to tell God some day, "If we had known it was you, Lord, we would have fed you . . . and given you clothes and shoes. We thought it was just a bunch of bums. . . . We didn't know it was you, Lord."[4]

Soon the workload was too heavy for Marie. It was then she discovered Doris Nye, a young college graduate who was singing with a Lutheran church group. Doris hoped to become a missionary to South America, but when she discovered that she could help Marie with her work, she began right then and there. She moved in with Marie and the two became fast friends. Doris brought many talents to her work: gifts in music, executive ability, and a kind and compassionate nature. "God always sends the best," Marie said of Doris. They were to stay together a lifetime.

In 1948 the two women were threatened with eviction. The owner wanted to sell the building to a liquor dealer. Marie and Doris sent out letters to all the friends of the mission. Enough money poured in so that they bought the whole building.

"The slums and ghettos are needy mission fields," Marie said. "Many churches have been occupied with other lands. Another world. Another time. And have not been aware of the needs in the city's backyards and side streets. 'While they slept the enemy came and sowed tares.' Drink. Drugs. Broken windows. Burned buildings."[5] But the door of the mission always welcomed the homeless and hungry. Most other doors, except for the taverns, were closed to them.

One of the miracles of the mission was 86-year-old Dad Annis. "Dad" was the name often given to older men who helped at the mission. As a young man, Fred Annis had decided that he wanted no part of religion. He thought it was too restrictive, so he made one bad choice after another. He ended up in trouble with the law and spent more than sixty years in and out of the workhouse or on the streets.

One night Fred stumbled into Marie's mission. As he listened to the songs and prayers of his childhood, and heard the story of Jesus' love, the hard exterior of his heart began to crumble. At last he decided to let God take over his life.

From that time until his death two years later, Dad Annis changed dramatically. During those last years he proclaimed the good news to all his buddies. He would stand in the middle of a cheap Skid Row coffee shop and thunder to his listeners, "Jesus saves. He saved me, a drunkard, a bum, and a no-good. Jesus loves me and he loves you too."

At 88 years of age, Dad Annis was hospitalized. As he lay near death, he spoke to Marie and Doris with wonder and anticipation in his voice. "I will be in heaven before tomorrow morning," he said with a smile. "But don't worry about me. I am going to have a wonderful time with the One who died for me." That night Dad Annis died peacefully. The hospital chaplain called Marie and Doris at midnight. "Fred Annis just passed away whispering, 'Come Lord Jesus.'"

The mission hall was packed for the funeral. People wept during the closing hymn:

> Safe in the arms of Jesus,
> Safe from corroding care;
> Safe from the world's temptations,
> Sin cannot harm me there.[6]

Dad Annis was safely home with God.

John, a bartender on Washington Avenue, spent more time inside the workhouse than outside tending bar. He was always in some kind of trouble or other. One day, just after being released from jail, he began wandering down Washington Avenue, and soon he was drunk again. In the evening he headed for his old hangout, Angelo's Bar. But when he arrived, he saw a cross shining where the old liquor sign had been.

John remembered the book he had read in high school, *Pilgrim's Progress,* in which the main character, Christian, lost his burden at the cross. John felt weighed down by the heavy burden he carried. With shaky steps, he went into the mission and up to the altar. "God be merciful to me a sinner," he cried aloud, "and save me for Jesus' sake." John felt a load lift from his heart. He pulled the wine bottle from his pocket and set it on the altar. He said earnestly, "Lord, I don't need this anymore." He asked Marie for a Bible. Hugging it to himself he declared, "Now this shall be my companion." John's new life in Christ gave him courage and strength to live and he became a tireless worker for the mission.

One day Marie's fellowship meeting was interrupted by a woman who rushed in sobbing. "My God! My God! Lock me up. I am afraid of myself! Lock me up!" She had been on her way to the bridge that spanned the Mississippi River. Once there, she planned to jump off and end it all. Suddenly she heard a familiar song coming from somewhere. "Take the name of Jesus with you, child of sorrow and of woe." The woman followed the sound until she saw the lighted cross which brought her into the mission. With love, the workers helped her understand how Jesus could make her life worth living. She went home renewed, and in time, influenced her husband to begin a new chapter of his life too.

One evening near midnight, Marie and Doris were driving across a bridge when they saw a young man preparing to jump off. They stopped the car. "We have a rescue mission just up the street," Marie told him. "You will feel better after a hot cup of coffee and some motherly counsel."

The young man, Bob, went with the women and confessed that he could not face himself anymore, or life without Addie. They had been married only three years with big dreams for their life together. Now Addie was through with him because of his deceitfulness.

Marie and Doris knew well that when people were desperate and at the end of their own strength, God could take over their lives. After coffee, talk, and prayers, they took Bob to a hotel room where Addie sat on the bed with tears running down her cheeks, a loaded gun nearby. She couldn't face another day either.

Marie and Doris helped the couple see that God could mend their brokenness. As they knelt to pray, Bob and Addie poured out their hearts to God. After hearing words of forgiveness and hope, they embraced and promised God and each other they would try again. In time the pair became missionaries to South America and continued their witness to God's saving power.

The Gateway mission kept expanding its programs to help men, women, and children until urban development finally forced them to move twice—first to Nicollet Island and then, in 1968, to 1112 East Franklin Avenue, an area with a high violent crime rate. There it has become known as the Marie Sandvik Center. The mission is still located there and continues to be a refuge for people of all ages. Each day the center buzzes with activity: breakfasts all summer, several children's clubs, vacation Bible school, women's meetings, a women's shelter, holiday celebrations, meals and clothing, evening services, and always the good news of the gospel. The center receives no government funds, because, as Marie believed, "The Lord's work should be supported by the Lord's people."

A big part of the center's energy concentrates on children. One day a little boy was sitting in a restaurant with his mother when suddenly he began pulling on his mother's shirt and pointing. "Sandpick's here! Sandpick's here!" he called excitedly. As Marie Sandvik approached the mother and child's table, the little boy pulled up his T-shirt and pointed to his heart. "God is there! And you put him there, Sandpick." The boy had learned of God's love at the breakfast club. The mother, too, had become a Christian after receiving help at the women's shelter and attending services at the center.

Sometimes the children become missionaries to their own families. One day a woman from a local church stopped by the center with her arms full of Christmas gifts from her women's group. "Do you remember a little girl named Ingeborg who used to live in that awful apartment?" she asked. Yes, Marie and Doris remembered. It was Christmas and little Ingeborg's mother was drinking as usual. Someone from the center stopped by, picked up Ingeborg and brought her to the mission. That night Ingeborg had a good dinner and heard the Christmas story. She received her first Christmas gifts, a knitted cap and mittens.

"I am Ingeborg's mother. Little Ingeborg came home that night and showed me her gifts. She told me that Jesus loved us. It broke my heart. I knelt to pray and promised God I'd live a new life. Today Ingeborg has her own family, teaches Sunday school, and has a prayer group in her home."[7]

Marie and Doris faced many difficult times. They were threatened with guns and knives, sworn at, and insulted, and the premises were robbed and vandalized. Would Marie spend another half century in this kind of work if she could live her life all over? "I'd do it all over again," said the woman who was active until her death, close to ninety years of age. "Ya, I would.

"Yes, the slum is a dismal place," said Marie. "And yet in its midst there is a light which continues to shine. Seven days a week, every day in the month, 365 days in the year. Our mission tells the story of the Christ who is able to save from the 'guttermost to the uttermost.' "[8]

Notes

1. Marie Sandvik and Doris Nye, *To the Slums with Love* (Minneapolis: Marie Sandvik Center, 1976), 19.

2. Christopher Phillips, "An Angel of Skid Row," St. Paul *Pioneer Press Dispatch, Parade,* Sunday, 7 July 1985), 10.

3. Joe Kimball, "Helping Those Who 'Don't Have a Grandmother,' " Minneapolis *Star and Tribune, Picture,* Sunday, 4 Sept. 1983), 9.

4. Marie Sandvik and Doris Nye, *To the Slums with Love,* 23.

5. Ibid., 23.

6. W. Howard Doane, "Safe in the Arms of Jesus," *Concordia: A Collection of Hymns and Spiritual Songs* (Minneapolis: Augsburg, 1922), #133.

7. Marie Sandvik and Doris Nye, "Christmas Newsletter," 1990.

8. Sandvik and Nye, *To the Slums with Love,* 45.

7 *William Booth*   1829–1912

The Rev. Samuel Dunn began the Sunday evening worship service at Broad Street Chapel with the opening prayer. Shadows from the gas-jet lights played along the wall. Seated in England's Nottingham congregation were shopkeepers, mill owners, and well-dressed women. However, many of the best seats facing the pulpit were empty. Pewholders paid their money to reserve their seats, and should they decide to attend services, their seats were ready and waiting.

Some latecomers entered, shuffling their feet. A portly mill owner opened one eye and looked toward the partition that separated the newly arrived from the rest of the congregation. He himself had contributed toward the buying of that partition. Yes, he nodded complacently, it was good that the unwashed street people sat behind an obstruction when they wished to worship. From there they could hear the service in progress, although they could not see. That was the way it should be. Why should the riffraff of society distract proper worshipers? The partition helped screen off a little of the body odor as well.

The prayer ended, and the minister seated himself on his red, plush chair. The congregation began singing "Rock of Ages." Voices soared and mingled with the shadows. They were just finishing the third stanza, "Foul I to the fountain fly . . ."

Suddenly the chapel door flew open. In strode a tall young man with a dark, black beard and a long nose; a motley group of street people followed him.

The worshipers nearly choked on their words. It was William Booth, known to all in Nottingham as Willful Will! Young William's jaw was firmly set as he led his group to the best seats in the church, the empty ones, facing the pulpit. The congregation could hardly sing verse four. How dare William bring these people—the scum—into this holy place, right where everyone was forced to look at them?

The rest of the service was pretty much lost to the majority in the congregation. All they could concentrate on was the scraggly bunch occupying those special seats.

Shopkeeper Albert Savery shifted in his pew. Secretly he admired the seventeen-year-old dynamic preacher with a heart for the poor. He knew that when William finished his long day working at the pawnshop, he set off for street corners and alleys to thunder and plead with the wayward. Albert could never forget the incident over Besom Jack, the broom seller. Jack was usually drunk early in the day. He beat his wife and was incorrigible and obnoxious to his neighbors and acquaintances.

One day Albert had an errand down on Kid Street, one of the worst areas in Nottingham. As he passed by Jack's hovel, he saw William standing on a chair right in front of Jack's door. Albert remembered his words well.

"Friends," said young William. "I want to put a few straight questions to your souls. Have any of you got a child at home without shoes to its feet? Are your wives sitting now in dark houses waiting for you to return without money?"

Besom Jack's door flew open and the red-faced broom seller staggered out. William went on preaching. "Are you going away from here to the public-houses to spend on drink, money that your wives need for food and your children for shoes?"[1]

Cursing, Besom Jack lunged at William, shouting, "You! Me wife's no concern o' yours!" The crowd perked up. A good fight would relieve the day's boredom.

"Jack," said William tenderly, "God loves your wife, and so did you, once. Can you remember how much you loved and cherished her when first you met?" Somehow the words soothed Jack. "Well, Jack," William continued, "God loves *you* with a love like that, with a love far deeper and greater than that."[2]

Jack searched William's face. "Me?" he asked incredulously.

William climbed off his chair and gently took Jack's arm. "Yes, Jack, you. Come Jack, just kneel down here and tell the Lord you love him too. And ask him to forgive you."[3]

Jack knelt, and prayed, and wept while the crowd watched with unbelieving eyes. Jack asked God's forgiveness and promised to change. God helping him, change he did. Jack quit drinking and began treating his wife tenderly. Everyone in town saw that Jack was a new person.

If William could succeed in reaching people like Jack so that they were changed by God, he could bring all the derelicts he wished into church as far as Albert Savery was concerned. The church was getting too stuffy anyhow—more concerned with rituals than with people's souls and needs.

Tonight's incident was far from over, however. A committee called upon William and warned that never again was he to bring such people in the front door at Broad Street Chapel.

Many years passed after the incident at Broad Street Chapel. William had finished theological training in London, married, begun a family, and served several parishes. By this time he was a successful preacher in Gateshead at a large congregation (nicknamed "The Converting Shop") which had grown from one hundred members to more than two thousand. William, however, was dissatisfied. His heart ached for those whom the established churches neglected and ignored. He was sure there was something more God wanted him to do.

William finally resigned his position, left the Methodist church, and went to work in the slums of London's East End, preaching salvation on every corner. It didn't take him long to decide that this was where his life's work must be: here, among these people with their enormous needs. He rushed home to tell Catherine, "Darling, I have found my destiny!"[4]

In the East End at that time (1865), every fifth shop was a gin shop. While parents lay drunk at home, little ones cried on the streets because they had no bread or warm clothes. Many owners built steps to the bar to make it easier for the littlest children to climb up and buy gin for a penny. Cirrhosis of the liver and delirium tremens were not uncommon among the young ones.

Besides drinking, people filled dreary hours by fighting in filth-laden streets and alleys and by prodding dogs into bloody battles. Hungry people prowled the area for rotten fruit or vegetables to eat. Sick and old people huddled together in miserable hovels or tenements without money for firewood or food. Many flats were so crowded that renters leased part of their rooms and slept in shifts. Some clergymen even excused such overcrowding with, "It keeps the poor snug in cold weather."[5]

Those who could get jobs, including very young children, worked twelve to sixteen hours a day in factories and other industries, laboring in dangerous and unhealthy conditions. There were no social organizations to help these desperate people secure food, clothing, jobs, medical aid, or child care. They were on their own, whatever their age, health, or ability.

Prostitution was the only way many women could feed and clothe themselves or their families. Child prostitution was big business with children being kidnapped or misled into the racket. Many poor families unwittingly sold their young daughters into such jobs. Women, dressed as nuns, lured trusting young Irish girls into the trade when they arrived in London from Liverpool, looking for work. Many houses of prostitution paid out bribes and provided free quarters for police detectives and constables.

Among such conditions, William and his coworkers saw that evil was no mere absence of good, but a fight "against the rulers, . . . authorities, . . . the cosmic powers of this present darkness . . . [and] spiritual forces of evil in the heavenly places" (Eph. 6:12).

Converts could not compromise their new lives with the old. A total conversion was necessary in order to fight the vicious enemy—an enemy that could easily pull them back into the gutter unless they were equipped with God's armor.

In the beginning years of his street ministry, persecution of William's followers was bitter: stoning, mudslinging, jeering, insults, and pelting with rotten eggs and fruit. Mobs kicked and charged workers, bloodied their faces, and heaved rocks through windows of meeting halls. Proprietors of sleazy businesses paid rabble-rousers to disturb William Booth's religious meetings. British Secret Service agents, too, disguised themselves at meetings and listened for seditious propaganda.

William's son, Bramwell, became angry at all the persecutions and hostility. William replied, "Bramwell, fifty years hence it will matter very little indeed how these people treated us. It will matter a great deal how we dealt with the work of God."[6]

William Booth believed, however, that talk was not enough. He began food programs for the poor and opened soup kitchens and shops that sold good meals at low cost. He said, "We cannot console empty bellies with promises of heavenly bliss. Remember Jesus' words, 'Give them to eat.' " Sixteen-year-old Bramwell Booth arose at 3:00 A.M. every morning and pushed a wheelbarrow four miles to the Covent Garden Market where be bought sacks of soup bones and begged for discarded vegetables. Then he pushed the wheelbarrow four miles back so soup could be made for hungry people.

William Booth's genius for organization and leadership provided the impetus for many social reforms. He began homes for the homeless and for released prisoners, safe houses for women and girls, legal aid for the poor, help for alcoholics, and an employment exchange which trained people to become self-supporting. Booth's army of workers also exposed the horrors in child prostitution which caused such a tumult that outraged people joined efforts to stamp out the evil. Although William's enemies tried to discredit his findings, the publicity pumped new vigor into the organization instead.

In 1878 the name Salvation Army was born. William had always been fascinated by military language, so the name seemed appropriate for this "hallelujah army" that was fighting for God and waging war on the devil and his angels.

Before long the Salvation Army spread around the world. Persecution diminished and the work of William Booth's organization was recognized by outstanding leaders in every country.

In spite of these successes, William never lost his common touch or concern for those outside the faith. After one rousing meeting, an aide said to Booth, "Wonderful, General. Did you see them? A hundred to the Penitent-form [kneeling bench] in ten minutes!"

William Booth answered solemnly, "I saw the hundreds going out, having rejected Christ."[7] To his diary he confided, "Trying to make people good is indeed a weary, disheartening business. I wonder why God has not given the world up long ago."[8]

Yet William never considered giving up either. He followed a vigorous schedule of travel and preaching until near the end of his life when he became blind. In his final speech he thundered to a rapt audience, "While women weep . . . I'll fight; while little children go hungry . . . I'll fight; while men go to prison . . . I'll fight; while there yet remains one dark soul without the light of God, I'll fight—I'll fight to the very end!"[9]

On his deathbed he pleaded to his son, "Bramwell, I want you to do more for the homeless . . . in every land. Ah, my boy, we don't know what it means to be without a home. Bramwell, look after the homeless. Promise me."[10]

Bramwell promised. He took his father's place as the new leader of the Salvation Army and continued to fight for human needs.

Notes

1.   Richard Collier, *The General Next to God: The Story of William Booth and The Salvation Army* (New York: E. P. Dutton & Co., 1965), 30.

2.   Jenty Fairbank, *William and Catherine Booth: God's Soldiers* (London: Hodder and Stoughton, 1974), 30.

3.   Ibid., 30.

4.   Collier, *The General,* 26.

5.   Ibid., 46.

6.   Ibid., 194.

7.   Ibid., 194.

8.   Edward Bishop, *Blood and Fire! The Story of General William Booth and The Salvation Army* (London: Longmans, Green and Co., 1964), 78.

9.   Collier, *The General,* 244.

10.   Ibid., 245.

8 *Catherine Mumford Booth*

1829–1890

Catherine was passing through the poor area of town as she hurried along to the Gateshead Methodist Chapel in London to hear her husband, William Booth, preach. Suddenly it seemed that a voice spoke to her. "Wouldn't you be doing God more service by inviting these poor folk to the chapel than by going to enjoy it yourself?"[1]

Catherine was frightened. Was the voice coming from her imagination, or was this really the voice of the Lord giving her instructions? She promised God she would try.

Just ahead was a woman sitting on some tenement steps with a jug in her hand. "Perhaps she's drunk," Catherine told herself, "and doesn't want to talk to me." But she didn't let herself off so easily.

"Would you like to go to the chapel with me?" Catherine forced herself to ask.

"Me?" asked the woman. She looked down at her shabby clothes and shook her head. "My drunken husband keeps me at home."

"I'd like to see your husband and talk to him," said Catherine.

"It's no use," answered the woman. "He's drunk and you won't be able to do anything with him. All he does is sit and drink."

Catherine persisted. Finally the woman led her into the dreary flat. Her husband, an intelligent-looking man of about forty, sat, drunk, with a jug resting on the floor by his chair. Gently Catherine began to talk to him, all the while trying to be sensitive to whatever direction God might give her. She spoke so clearly about the love of God that the man perked up and listened.

Then Catherine pulled out her Bible and read Jesus' account of the prodigal son. Absorbed, the man followed the story, and soon tears trickled down his face. "God loves you like that father," Catherine told him as she finished. That was the beginning of a change for the man and his wife. Within a few weeks, he and ten other alcoholics whom Catherine gathered together began attending Bible study and prayer together. Eventually all ten of them quit drinking.

On another Sunday morning God spoke to Catherine as she sat in the chapel service with her son, four-year-old Bramwell. The message seemed to be, "Now if you were to speak, you know I would bless it to your own soul, as well as to the people."[2]

Catherine was seized with fear, just as she had been when she first talked to the drunken husband. What if I make a fool of myself? she thought. Then she made a decision. "I have never yet been willing to be a fool for Christ. Now I *will* be one."[3]

Catherine left Bramwell in the pew and walked up the aisle to the pulpit. A murmur went through the congregation. Was Catherine ill? William wondered the same. Something must be very wrong with his wife to have her interrupt the service in this manner.

William came down from the pulpit. "What is the matter, my dear?" he asked.

"I want to say a word," Catherine replied.

William was quite surprised, but he turned to the congregation of one thousand people and said, "My dear wife wishes to speak." Then he sat down.

Catherine told the crowd that they may have thought she was an obedient Christian, but she wasn't at all. God was asking her to preach the good news of Jesus, too, as her husband did, but she did not do it because she was afraid. Catherine's eloquent speaking moved many people to tears. She finished by saying, "Now I have promised the Lord that, from this moment on, I will be obedient."[4]

As Catherine turned to sit down, William announced, "Tonight my wife will be the preacher." That evening the chapel was packed with people, some even sitting on the window sills.

This event began Catherine's career in preaching, along with an intense social ministry program. She was an intelligent, well-read woman with strong theological interests. As a child, she had read the Bible eight times before she was twelve.

At nine Catherine already showed deep compassion for the unfortunate and knew what Jesus expected of his followers. One sunny day that year, she was playing outside with a hoop and stick when suddenly a noisy crowd came surging along the road. In front a constable pulled and prodded a prisoner as the mob laughed, jeered, and insulted the humiliated man. Catherine immediately saw the prisoner's loneliness, without a friend in sight. *She* would be his friend. She ran over to the frightened man and walked beside him all the way to the lock-up.

Now, as a wife, preacher, and mother of a growing family, Catherine believed, as William did, that words must be backed up with deeds, and that the destiny for her and her husband lay in forsaking the respectable chapels and reaching out to the troubled masses. She helped poor mothers give birth, bathed their babies, and arranged for food, water, firewood, and shelter for the poor. She worked with drunkards, the aged, homeless wanderers, and carried out a ministry to prostitutes. At Christmas time she recruited help and cooked three hundred dinners to give away to the needy.

Catherine was a strong leader and a loving support to her husband, William, as he gave his life to the people in the slums of London. People criticized her because there were those who did not think it was fitting for a woman to preach or be busy outside the home. From the time she was a young woman, however, Catherine had believed that women were equal to men and nowhere did the Bible teach otherwise.

Catherine also raised her eight children to have caring hearts and encouraged them to have good behavior. After telling little Katie about some of the cruelty she saw in society she said, "And it's all because there's wickedness in the world, Katie. Do you know, little one, I would rather my boys grew up to be chimney-sweeps and my girls grew up to be scullery maids, than that they should grow up wicked."[5] Little as she was, Katie decided then that she *never* was going to be wicked.

Catherine instilled in her children a sense of mission as well. "Now Katie," she told her oldest, "you are not in this world for yourself. You have been sent for others. The world is waiting for you."[6]

This message stayed with Kate, and when she was twenty-two years old, she went to Paris to head up a campaign in the worst part of Paris. Before leaving, Catherine presented a French flag to her daughter, saying, "Carry it into the slums and alleys, everywhere there are lost and perishing souls, and preach under its shadow the everlasting gospel of Jesus Christ."[7]

For six months, Katie and her lieutenants tried to wage a war on "the world, the flesh, and the devil" at the Rue d' Angoulème, a hall in the Belleville slums. So far there had been six months of chaos. Night after night the crowds jeered and stirred up trouble. Roughs ripped out pages from the Bibles and lit their cigars. Female workers were pulled by their bonnet strings until they lost their breath. The police were as vindictive as the mobs. Although Katie felt like giving up, she remembered her mother's words, "Katie, you are not in this world for yourself."

One night everything was out of control, with the mob screaming, cursing, and jeering. Soon the activity escalated into a wild dance. Although Katie felt despair, she kept her wits and shouted at the tall, handsome ringleader named Emile. "Mes amis! I will give you twenty minutes to dance if you will give me twenty minutes to speak. Are you agreed?"[8]

He and the crowd agreed, and after twenty minutes of dancing, yelling, and hooting, Emile saw to it that Katie had her turn. As everyone sat down, they wondered what this female speaker could say to interest them. As she began her electrifying sermon, total silence settled over the hall. Twenty minutes went by, then forty, sixty, finally one hour and twenty minutes! When it was over, a thoughtful crowd filed out, all but Emile. He sat at the back of the auditorium, head in his hands. Quietly Katie walked up to him. "Thank you for helping me tonight."

"Do you have time to listen?" he asked in an anguished voice. Then he poured out his story. Once he had had a family that he dearly loved, but his wife lost her reason and was placed in an asylum. His cherished son died at six years of age and now he was alone. "Why did God let this happen to me if he loves me?"

"I do not know," answered Katie. "But I *do* know that God loves you."

"But I've hated him, and shaken my fist at the heavens. Can he ever forgive me?" asked Emile.

"It is certain," said Katie.

That night the bitter man let God begin to heal the hatred in his heart. The next night he stood before the crowd and testified to God's love and power. From that day on he became one of Kate's best helpers. Each night the crowds grew bigger and by the year's end Katie and her workers moved to a new hall which seated 1,200.

Catherine's teaching influenced another daughter: Evangeline (Eva). One day Eva went to check on "old Bob" who was bedridden. He lived in a rickety garret with filthy floors, broken stairs, and a warped door. Eva found that his fire was out and that he had only a thin strip of sacking to cover him. His cracked cup held dirty drinking water and he had not eaten for days.

The old man's eyes lit up when he saw Eva. "Please bring me my bread in the cupboard," he begged. Eva looked and found only one crust of dry bread. Old Bob was so excited by that miserable crust that he struggled to pull himself upright. Then he bowed his head and prayed, "Oh Lord, for what I am about to receive, make me truly thankful."[9]

Eva dissolved in tears, and rushed out to buy kindling and food. She scrubbed the old man's place and cooked him a hot meal—the first he had eaten in months.

Once Catherine and William feared that fiery Evangeline could satisfy her dramatic flair only by becoming an actress, but she found fulfillment in the Salvation Army. Eventually she became its National Commander in the United States. In charge of her spiritual "troops" in France during World War I, the organization won new respect for their powerful examples of caring and self-sacrifice.

Eva remembered when Bramwell, her brother, asked their father the secret of his strength. The elder Booth replied that as a young man he pledged to give God all there was of William Booth. But Eva added this postscript, "That wasn't really his secret—his secret was that he never took it back."[10]

Catherine Booth's ideas affected the entire Salvation Army structure. Her belief in the equality between men and women was apparent in many of the army's organizations where she placed women in command of men, a startling idea for that day. Catherine's influence was also seen in the *Orders and Regulations* for the Salvation Army which stated, "It must be borne in mind that women have talents which are not possessed by men, and neglect to call such talents into action . . . will result in the everlasting loss of the blessing they could have bestowed upon the world." Regulations also stated that, "A woman is not to be kept back from any position of power or influence merely on account of her sex."[11]

Catherine became known around the world as the "Salvation Army Mother." On her deathbed from cancer at age sixty-one, she wrote to friends, "Don't be concerned about your dying, only go on living well, and the dying will be all right."[12] And to her family she said, "Never think of me as in the grave."[13]

After Catherine's death the flags continued to fly at full mast, because to members of the Salvation Army, death is considered a promotion.

Notes

1. Jenty Fairbank, *William and Catherine Booth: God's Soldiers* (London: Hodder and Stoughton, 1974), 45.
2. Edward Bishop, *Blood and Fire! The Story of General William Booth and The Salvation Army* (London: Longmans, Green and Co., 1964), 47.
3. Richard Collier, *The General Next to God: The Story of William Booth and The Salvation Army* (New York: E. P. Dutton & Co., 1965), 41.
4. Fairbank, *God's Soldiers*, 50.
5. Ibid., 47.
6. Collier, *The General*, 57.
7. Fairbank, *God's Soldiers*, 100.
8. Ibid., 101.
9. Collier, *The General*, 182.
10. Ibid., 210.
11. Bishop, *Blood and Fire!* 87–88.
12. Collier, *The General*, 188.
13. Fairbank, *God's Soldiers*, 115.

9 *Robert Childress*   1890–1956

Bob Childress was troubled by the message B. B. Franklin brought him. "We need your help bad over in Indian Valley," Franklin said. "People ain't just a-killin' each other. They's a-killin' theirselves, and we ain't got a pastor. The soul sickness is gettin' real big. Please come."

Pastor Childress was already very busy in his far-flung parish on Buffalo Mountain in the Blue Ridge Mountains of Virginia. The problems among his own people were overwhelming enough. For generations these rugged descendants of Scotch-Irish immigrants had lived on Buffalo Mountain. The surrounding hills hemmed them in and left them isolated from the rest of the world, along with their fear, ignorance, and superstition. The people were proud of their land, their customs and language. They firmly believed in their right to make their own whiskey and settle their scores with guns, knives, or rocks. Little boys as young as six or eight learned to use a gun, and every lad's ambition was to wear long pants, carry a gun, and be feared.

As B. B. Franklin waited for a reply, Bob knew that if he didn't go to Indian Valley, his conscience would gnaw at him. The Valley was close by, and he decided he must try and squeeze in the needs of that community with his own. "Of course I'll come," he told Franklin.

Later, Bob Childress looked up at the bulging hump of Buffalo Mountain. He remembered when he graduated from seminary, an official of the Presbytery had said, "There is no more violent, troubled land in all the southern mountains of America. They're an island untouched by change." Bob turned down a well-established, financially secure church for the poverty of these mountains. But Bob had grown up here, and he understood the land and the people of the Blue Ridge.

He had been a pastor on the Buffalo for four years by this time, and some days he thought that at last things were changing for the better; then a new victim would be shot or lie dead from a stabbing. Liquor was the root of so much anguish, yet bootleggers continued to hide their stills in the wooded hills and carry on a brisk business day and night.

Bob Childress figured that Indian Valley, at least, would give him some new problems to work on, so he began driving over there every Sunday night to hold services. His fun-loving nature, ready laughter, and storehouse of jokes were a welcome change in this solemn territory. "More laughter and fun are needed around here," Bob said. He told the people that they could find more excitement in serving the Lord than in fighting, feuding, and getting drunk.

Two Indian Valley drinking buddies, Wyatt and Blaine, were so fond of their new preacher that they drank to his success. Wyatt began hiking miles, sometimes as many as fifteen, to hear Bob preach. It wasn't long before both men saw the empty futility of the way they lived and asked to be baptized. The ceremony took place at midnight following a prayer meeting. Afterwards Blaine confessed, "I'm a boozehound, and I just can't stop drinking!"

"Blaine," said Bob, "you'll just have to start spending your time learning some better habits, like going to church and teaching Sunday school and working longer hours in the field. You stop your bad habits by keeping so busy with good ones that there's no more time for the bad ones. 'Nature hates a vacuum,' they say."[1]

Since drinking was such a big problem all over the Blue Ridge, Bob began preaching against liquor from the pulpit. Hobert Quesenberry, Blaine's younger brother, was another man troubled by drink. People in the valley said Hobert had been marked with liquor before he was born and that's why he couldn't throw it off.

Many in the community had given up on Hobert long ago, but Bob never gave up on anybody. He saw Hobert as an able person and a good family man when he was sober. Lately the sober times were becoming fewer and fewer. Hobert was drinking so heavily that soon the family's money was gone. Then Hobert began gambling and ended up losing his job and his credit.

On top of it all, Hobert was about to lose the farm he rented from his father-in-law, Wyatt Hylton. Wyatt didn't think his son-in-law could be depended on to manage the debt so he was about to sell to a buyer who wanted immediate possession of the place. There was nothing left for Hobert, his wife, Bertha, and the four children to do but to move, and they had nowhere to go. Not one of his many brothers or sisters would help him out because their faith in him was gone.

Moving day arrived for the Quesenberrys. Hobert looked about, a lump in his throat. The garden was all planted, and the apple trees were blossoming. Hobert loved this place, and he wanted to do better for his family. He just couldn't help himself. Then Bob Childress stopped by. It seemed that Bob always knew when someone was in trouble or about to be in trouble. "Come on, Hobert," he said. "We're going over to Wyatt's place."

"It's no use, Mr. Childress," Hobert told him. "My daddy-in-law wants five hundred now."

Bob told him, "Anyone who can shoot squirrels the way you can ought to be good for five hundred dollars. Let's go!"[2]

Bob and Hobert drove to see Wyatt first, then headed for the bank in town. "How much money do I have in my account?" Bob asked the teller.

"Thirty-five dollars, Mr. Childress."

"Do you suppose I can write out a check for five hundred dollars?" asked Bob.

Bob Childress was well known at the bank. He had signed notes before so people wouldn't lose their homes or farms. He talked mightily for the little guy who needed a loan but who never would have gotten it on his own reputation. And he always made good the credit he owed. The teller handed Bob the five-hundred note which he signed in his big, jagged handwriting. The two men drove back to the farm and when Hobert saw it he said, "It's not so much to anyone else, but to me it looks like paradise."

Hobert was so moved by Bob's faith in him that he began fighting the liquor urge in earnest. He got a job tending a boiler for a dollar a day, but every hour he fought the battle with liquor, and many times he lost. He felt so low because Bob was the only person who had faith in him and he was letting him down. He drank harder.

Bob checked on Hobert often to see how things were going. He'd stop by to tell a story, to swap something, to help Hobert shoot rabbits for the orphanage, or to borrow a tool. He always found an excuse to visit.

Bob understood the struggle Hobert was having. How well he remembered! It was years ago now. At twenty he himself drank so much that he was rarely sober.

One day Bob's big brother, Hasten, a tough fighter and heavy drinker, came home and said, "Bob, I believe drink is bad. It makes a little man biggety and big man a fool. I believe I'll give it up."[3]

But Bob kept right on drinking, brawling, and fighting with rocks, knives, and guns, and he had scars to show for it. One day he survived a brutal melee and started to walk six miles home. "Isn't there more to life," he wondered, "than being drunk, playing poker, throwing rocks at your enemies, and feuding with guns and knives?" For the past few days he had been so drunk that he hadn't eaten a decent meal and his stomach turned nearly inside out with agony. He hated himself.

As he shuffled along, he heard singing. He wondered how he had arrived at the little church. Filled with liquor he couldn't quite figure out where his feet were taking him. He found himself staggering into the service and listening to the revival preaching. Before he knew it, he went forward for the altar call. As he knelt at the altar rail, peace began to enter his confused heart and still his anguish. Quietly he slipped out of the church, went home, and slept soundly for the first time in months without any brandy.

Bob went back to the church again the next night with his cousin. On the way home he felt the urge to pray with his cousin, and Jess confessed, "People think I'm tough and dangerous, but I'm really a coward inside. I've never dared tell anyone, but I'm so sick of myself that I can't stay sober."

Later Bob said, "That week of revival didn't change me into a new man, but it gave me the first real peace in my whole life. For the first time I had felt a power stronger than the power of liquor and rocks and guns."[4]

Bob remembered this struggle now as he tried to help Hobert through his ups and downs. There was even a time when Hobert's drinking made him so impossible that Bertha took the children and came to stay with the Childress family.

One evening something happened to Hobert. "I was a'lyin' there on that couch," he said later, "when all of a sudden it came to me. I had to see the preacher. Seemed I couldn't get to him fast enough. I told Bertha I had to join the church. She gottened a neighbor to take me to him. I could barely whisper, but I had to talk with him."[5]

Pastor Childress helped Hobert wrestle with his inner turmoil until his head cleared and he surrendered his life to God. A prayer meeting was held in Hobert's own house and that night he was baptized. Joyful people from the community came to witness the event. From that day on, Hobert gave up the drinking.

Hobert said that afterwards there were always people who tried to get him to start in again. One night he was caught in pouring rain and chilled to the bone. A man at the mill tried to warm him up with a drink. Hobert was really tempted, but he told the man, "The Bible says, 'Woe unto him that giveth his neighbor drink' " (Hab. 2:15). The man never bothered Hobert again.

At last Hobert and Bertha started paying back the debt they owed to Bob Childress, five dollars at a time. "The more we paid back," Hobert said, "the easier it gottened."

Neither Bob nor Hobert knew what had really happened to send Hobert to Bob Childress that night. But down the road lived Mrs. Thurman Harris, a woman who had deep concern for Hobert. "There wasn't a day but what I prayed for him," she said. "I'd known him from school days on up, and for years he was the first one in my prayers. One day he came over, drunk as a barred owl. I'll never forget it. He was weaving down the road, his head on his chest, his shoes untied, and stumbling over the laces, and it hit me, 'What's the use of praying for a man like that all these years?' But right away it seemed I had a strong answer, that something would happen. I don't like to tell about it much; when I hear people say these things I feel sort of embarrassed for them. Anyway, I told my husband that I thought Hobert was going to get well. It wasn't but a few hours until the news came."[6]

Pastor Childress helped out at Indian Valley for about two years until a new minister came and during that time changes were happening all over the valley. Bob's lively sense of humor, his persistence, and the way he cared for every person had transformed the lives of many ornery and defeated individuals.

Bob continued his hectic pace in his own parish on the Buffalo. He drove an average of 40,000 miles a year on roads that many thought were impassable. He gathered food for the hungry, picked up derelicts along the road and took them home, drove people to the doctor or to town for medicine, visited those in trouble, paid lock-up fines for young men in jail, and kept preaching what the Bible said about changing one's ways, loving the neighbor, and looking out for each other.

When Pastor Childress visited people in their homes and invited them to church, they had a hard time saying no because he had a solution to every excuse. He would help them find proper clothes, pick them up at church time, or hold services at their house if they were sick.

Bob was threatened time and again by bootleggers. They set up roadblocks against him when he drove home at night. Repeatedly, rocks were thrown at church windows during his services, and his followers lived in fear that he would be the next one shot. He was a big man and not easily intimidated. He threw many troublemakers out on their ears and faced menacing situations with humor and toughness.

For those who were fighting the liquor urge, he sometimes stopped by with a shotgun and suggested they hunt squirrels together. Or he would invite them to come hear him preach, or get in the car and go along for a little drive. He complimented people, encouraged them, and involved them in projects. Most of all, he made everybody feel important and valued. In time, with the help of the Holy Spirit, Bob Childress moved mountains of ignorance, suspicion, and hatred, and pumped new life and hope into the community.

Bob never regretted the difficult decision to become a minister. Back when his little son began first grade, Bob had started high school, ten years older than all the other students. He finished in record time, then had gone on to college and seminary. With high marks and recommendations he was able to accomplish what everyone thought at first would be impossible because he had come from an impoverished and limited background, was poor, and also had a wife and growing family besides.

Bob Childress finally died because he couldn't slow down; people had many things to say about him.

Hazel Bowman: "If I'm worth anything, it's because of Mr. Childress. He changed my life."

Miss Blanche Green, a schoolteacher: "I used to sit and look at him and think, if you only knew how many lives you've transformed!"

Old Doc Burnett: "He was the savior of the Buffalo. And a sort of Robin Hood, too, getting donations from his rich friends and passing them along to the poor ones."

Josephine Mayberry: "I'm tryin' to live so I can see him agin someday . . ."[7]

When his casket was lowered into the ground, two old mountaineers were in no hurry to leave the scene. "Now Bob Childress is gone," said one. "You won't have another Bob Childress. There just won't be another."

The other answered, "There won't never need to be."[8]

Notes

1.   Richard C. Davids, *The Man Who Moved a Mountain* (Philadelphia: Fortress Press, 1970), 173.

2.   Ibid., 175.

3.   Ibid., 29.

4.   Ibid., 30.

5.   Ibid., 177.

6.   Ibid., 177.

7.   Ibid., 249.

8.   Ibid., 250.

10 *Florence Nightingale* 1820–1910

Florence was bored and miserable. Teas, embroidery, carriage rides in the afternoon, empty-headed conversation about clothes and propriety. Gossip about neighbors and relatives. Endless review of problems concerning the cook or butler. Incessant fuss over the selection of new apparel or furnishings and a constant round of parties. Wasn't there more to life than this?

Growing up in wealthy circumstances, Florence and her sister, Parthenope, had every material advantage as well as a fine private education. The family owned two elegant homes, Lea Hurst in the north of England and Embley in the south.

As Florence grew older she became more and more disgusted with her affluent lifestyle. In one letter she wrote, "I craved for some regular occupation, for something worth doing instead of frittering time away on useless trifles."[1]

Florence's mother, Fanny, was driven by social ambition. When Flo was sixteen and Parthe seventeen, they were soon ready to be launched into society, but Embley, in Fanny's mind, was not grand enough for such an event. Six more bedrooms must be added to the present nine. New kitchens were a necessity, and both the exterior and interior needed renovation.

The family decided to travel abroad while the remodeling of Embley took place. In the midst of all the packing commotion, something unusual happened to Florence on February 7, 1837. She received a call from God! The call was not merely an idea in her mind, but clearly a voice from outside herself. The voice did not tell her what course of action to take, but it did call her into God's service.

In September the Nightingales finally set off on their European tour which lasted a year and a half. The family rented sumptuous quarters and spent time at balls, parties, and banquets. They saw cathedrals and art museums, attended concerts and receptions. Florence shone in discussions and conversations and was admired and respected for her brilliance. As the family returned to England, Florence began to think again about the call from the Lord. Why hadn't God spoken again? She could only conceive that her frantic social life had blotted out God.

When the Nightingales reached home, Embley was not yet finished, so the family went to London for the season. In the glittering social life of London, Florence and Parthenope were presented at court and a new round of parties and balls began. With all the activity, it seemed to Florence that God's call faded again.

Finally home at Embley, Fanny continued the frenzied social life. She was especially proud of beautiful, intelligent, graceful Florence. Florence, however, did not feel satisfied with others' high opinions of her. In a private note she wrote, "All I do is done to win admiration."[2] She reminded herself that she would never be worthy of God's call unless she conquered her quest for praise and approval.

Completely oblivious to Florence's inner turmoil, Fanny continued her lavish spending and devoted all her energy into making the family's social status shine. Florence, however, was increasingly aware of the misery outside her spoiled and comfortable social circle. It was 1842, the "hungry forties" in England. People were starving and out of work and labor conditions were atrocious. Multitudes were sick, poor, and ignorant, and the workhouses, prisons, and hospitals were filled to capacity. In a private note Florence wrote, "My mind is absorbed with the idea of the sufferings of man, it besets me behind and before . . . all that poets sing of the glories of this world seems to me untrue. All the people I see are eaten up with care or poverty or disease."[3]

Florence began to sense that God wanted her to work to relieve the suffering of the world, but how to do so was still a mystery. "What can I do to lift the load of suffering from the miserable and helpless masses?" she asked herself. With these thoughts tumbling through her mind, Florence increased her visits to the villages. She begged her mother for medicine, food, bedding, clothes, and other supplies for the miserable poor.

Florence's obsession with the poor and orphaned annoyed her mother. Although Fanny was generous in her own charity giving, she tried to block many of her daughter's efforts, and conflicts between the two escalated. On top of that, relatives were badgering Flo to accept a marriage proposal. She finally broke under the emotional strain and took to her bed. While despairing over her life, she came to a secret decision. Her destiny lay in ministering to the sick.

"Hospital" and "nurse" had horrible connotations in 1845. Hospitals were crowded, dirty, foul-smelling places. Waste matter covered the wooden floors, and patients lay on filthy mattresses and bedding. Fights broke out frequently as patients battled for smuggled gin and brandy to ease their pain.

Most nurses were women of bad character. Many were also prostitutes and drunkards. Florence knew her family would forbid her to pursue a career in such a place, so she must think of a way to do it on her own.

Another year dragged by with round after round of parties. During much of the feverish activity, Florence was confined to her bed, an emotional wreck. She wrote in her private notes, "When one thinks there are hundreds and thousands of people suffering . . . when one sees in every cottage some trouble which defies sympathy—and there is all the world putting on its shoes and stockings every morning all the same—and the wandering earth going its inexorable treadmill through those cold hearted stars, in the eternal silence, as if nothing were the matter; death seems less dreary than life at that rate."[4]

Ironically, serious illness in others rescued Florence from a mental breakdown. After nursing her ailing grandmother and tending the sick and dying in the village, she realized that training in nursing skills was essential, but so far the only requirement for a nurse was that she be a woman. Florence had noted much ignorance in nursing care. She wrote to a friend, "I saw a poor woman die before my eyes this summer because there was nothing but fools to sit up with her, who poisoned her as much as if they had given her arsenic."[5]

Finally she knew what she must do. She would become a nurse. There was an infirmary a short distance away where she hoped to begin. But when she told her family about her plan, Fanny and Parthenope became hysterical. Florence's father, William Edward, took off for London, disgusted because he had spent time and money educating his beautiful daughters and now in his opinion, Florence was acting spoiled and ungrateful. Florence felt helpless and defeated. She wrote to a friend, "No advantage that I can see comes of my living on, excepting that one becomes less and less of a young lady every year . . . no one but the mother of it knows how precious an infant idea becomes; nor how the soul dies, between the destruction of one and the taking up of another. I shall never do anything and am worse than dust and nothing. . . . Oh for some strong thing to sweep this loathsome life into the past."[6]

As Florence despaired of her tiresome life, she was sure her suffering was God's punishment for her sins. She was plagued with guilt and indecision, and felt suffocated by her parents' control. She begged God to let her die.

Fortunately, her strong sense of determination saved her. To survive the insufferable routine at home, she began studying hospital reports and public health issues. She arose before daybreak and read by candlelight. She also filled notebook after notebook with facts, figures, and reports on hospital conditions in Europe and England.

After breakfast she carried out her assigned chore of organizing the family linens, glassware, silver, and china. Why do reasonable people want so many material goods? she wondered.

By chance, Florence heard of the Institution of Deaconesses at Kaiserswerth in Germany, a strict, disciplined religious institution with dedicated nuns who trained others in nursing. Such a place should meet the objections of her family. When she had the opportunity to visit hospitals and charitable institutions in Berlin and check out Kaiserswerth, she suddenly felt rich and vital. Nothing could stop her now.

However, when her family found out where she had been, Fanny went into a hysterical rage and Parthe collapsed in bed. In spite of them, Florence eventually went to Kaiserswerth. Life there was simple, the work hard, and the devotional life austere, but Florence loved it. She wrote to Fanny, "I find the deepest interest in everything here and am so well in body and mind. . . . Now I know what it is to live and to love life . . . I wish for no other earth, no other world than this."[7]

The short time at Kaiserswerth was soon over. Florence planned next to train at one of the great London hospitals, but again family obligations stood in the way. In her personal notes she wrote, "Oh weary days—oh evenings that seem never to end—for how many years have I watched that drawing-room clock and thought it never would reach the ten! And for twenty, thirty years more to do this!"[8]

Florence's despair finally turned to rebellion after the ridiculous treatment she received from her family during the social season in London. Although Florence had a very distinguished group of friends (George Eliot, Elizabeth Barrett Browning, Lord Shaftesbury, and others), her mother controlled her movements, read her mail, and supervised her invitations. Wasn't there any place in England where she could escape and use her talents and abilities?

The next years were like a seesaw. Florence's career path was blocked again and again. She packed and unpacked her trunks dozens of times while Fanny had tantrums and Parthe claimed to be near death on account of her sister. As Florence alternately acquiesced and rebelled, she nearly broke down herself.

Florence finally took a superintendent position in 1853 in London at The Institution for the Care of Sick Gentlewomen in Distressed Circumstances. The place was in chaos with no essential equipment on hand for furnishing the hospital. Florence faced the challenge with enthusiasm. Her organized, disciplined mind and creative imagination turned the place upside down with new standards of cleanliness and order. She arranged to have hot water piped to each floor, installed a dumbwaiter, bells in patients' rooms, and other improvements that had the entire place running so smoothly that even her opponents began singing her praises. Although Fanny still disapproved, she sent weekly hampers filled with flowers, vegetables, fruit, and meat for the patients.

During the sixteen years of waiting to discover how to answer to God's call, Florence had been shaped into the steel of genius. She wrote in a private note on January 1, 1854, "I have never repented nor looked back, not for one moment. And I begin the New Year with more true feeling of a happy New Year than I ever had in my life."[9] An acquaintance said of her abilities, "She stands perfectly alone, half-way between God and his creatures."[10]

In 1854 the Crimean War broke out between England and Russia. Britain's wounded poured into the medical complex at Scutari, Turkey, but there were no decent provisions for the soldiers. The army was badly organized and the patients were without essential supplies. The outraged citizens of England heard about the miserable state of their fighting men and demanded action. The secretary of war decided there was one woman in all England capable of organizing the medical chaos in Scutari: Florence Nightingale. Suddenly her name became known all over the country, and even her family gave their blessing to her call.

Florence gathered nurses and medical supplies and set sail for Scutari. Conditions there were even worse than she imagined. Wounded soldiers were crammed in filthy barracks which reeked from open sewers. Vermin crawled on the floors, and for a while the water supply flowed through the carcass of a dead horse. There were few cooking utensils, no bandages or medicine, and not enough mattresses, blankets, or other essentials. Hundreds of mutilated men poured in daily, frostbitten, ragged, and starving, and there was no room for them. Here was a task equal to Florence's genius.

Florence found the medical and military authorities to be hostile. Nurses had never been allowed on the battlefield before, and worse, the secretary of war had placed a female in charge of army medical affairs. They tried to block her efforts, but as they became overwhelmed with the wounded from Crimea, they grudgingly discovered that gentle Florence was also efficient, highly organized, and a strict disciplinarian to her nurses. In short order she untangled the cumbersome red tape that held up needed supplies, set up kitchens to cook nourishing food, furnished the soldiers with clothing and laundry services, and cleaned the buildings and water supply.

Before Florence came the barracks were full of cursing and crude talk. Under her influence the atmosphere became "holy as a church." She was often on her feet twenty hours at a time, bandaging the wounded, comforting them, consoling the dying, and writing messages to their families. At night she carried her lamp as she made rounds to check on her "children." The soldiers loved her and often kissed her shadow as it passed.

Late into the night she prepared long reports and recommendations to government and military authorities. Under her leadership the death rate in the hospitals dropped from 420 per thousand in February of 1855 to twenty-two per thousand in June of that year.

After her return to England, some people urged Florence to rest, but she answered, "I stand at the altar of the murdered men, and while I live I fight the cause."[11] She said that thousands of her children (soldiers) lay dead and forgotten in their graves from causes that could have been prevented. "But I can never forget."[12]

With contributions she established the Nightingale School to train nurses and develop character. "It must be," Florence wrote in 1875, "a home—a place of moral, religious and practical training—a place of training of character, habits and intelligence, as well as of acquiring knowledge."[13] Florence emphasized the spiritual nature of the nursing profession. She wanted her nurses to be not only highly skilled and efficient, but to sense the presence of God in their work as well. By the time Florence died in 1910 at the age of ninety, thousands of schools all over the world were dedicated to training nurses. God's call had been answered.

Notes

1.   Cecil Woodham-Smith, *Florence Nightingale* (London: McGraw-Hill, 1951), 9.

2. Ibid., 29.
3. Ibid., 31.
4. Ibid., 34.
5. Ibid., 38.
6. Ibid., 38–39.
7. Ibid., 61.
8. Ibid., 62.
9. Ibid., 77.
10. Ibid., 80.
11. Ibid., 181.
12. Ibid., 180.
13. Ibid., 335.

11 *Robert Raikes* 1736–1811

"There goes Bobby Wild Goose again with his ragged regiment! He's always up to something." A woman with a woolen shawl over her shoulders nodded emphatically as she exclaimed to the others standing with her near St. Mary de Crypt Cathedral in Gloucester. The group watched as Robert Raikes, trailed by a group of boys, left the church after 7:00 morning prayer.

"He's a buckish sort of man," commented a stout observer. "He dresses so showy, and look at him swagger."

"He may be vain," added a congenial woman, "but seeing is believing. Remember how the children used to go begging all over the streets every Sunday, cursing, swearing, and sticking each other with shawl pins, until Mr. Raikes got ahold of them. Now they follow him to church and they're neat and clean and well-behaved."

"But why does he do it?" asked a man leaning on his walking stick. "There must be something in it for him. People in England don't pay attention to poor ragamuffins without a good reason. Besides, all this learning will just make them proud and idle."

"Well let me tell you something," said a woman suspiciously, narrowing her eyes. "Mrs. Hannah More, a friend of Mr. Raikes, tried to form a Sunday school in the Cheddar district. And do you know why none of the parents allowed their children to attend? It's because Mrs. More really wanted the children to come to her school so she could sell them as slaves beyond the sea in the West Indies!"

Eyes of the listeners widened. After a few more exchanges the group drifted apart, still discussing their opinions of Raikes—some for and some against.

Several other neighborhood spectators watched Mr. Raikes walk along the street with his charges. He was a good-looking man dressed in a claret coat. His buff waistcoat had silver-gilt buttons and cambric frills and cuffs. He wore breeches, white stockings, and buckles on his shoes. A brown wig with a double row of curls covered his head, topped by a three-cornered hat. In his hand he carried a walking stick. The onlookers stared until "Bobby Wild Goose" was out of sight.

Robert first became interested in developing Sunday schools when he visited some businessmen in a slum of the city. There he saw children playing in the dirty streets, noisily milling about. When he asked about them, someone told him, "You should see them around here on a Sunday when they're all out from work at the factories. They curse, swear, riot. They tear up people's gardens and destroy property. Their parents don't pay any attention to them."

An idea began forming in Robert's mind. Would a school on Sundays be the answer, where the children could learn about religion, cleanliness, orderliness, and how to read? It didn't seem right to Robert that only the rich could go to school. He remembered the Bible words, "Train children in the right way." Perhaps this would solve the problem of so much crime among the young.

Since Mr. Raikes was the proprietor and editor of the *Gloucester Journal,* he frequently wrote his opinions on the need to educate children. In 1783 it had not occurred to anyone that educating children might be the state's responsibility. Raikes believed that the conditions of society produced criminals. Therefore, he reasoned, society punished what it manufactured. For years Mr. Raikes preached that intervening early in the lives of young troublemakers might prevent them from ending up in prison and on the gallows. But no one was ready to listen or act.

Robert Raikes decided he must do something himself. He recruited several women to help him begin his Sunday school in Sooty Alley. Sooty Alley was a good location for a school. It was near the Cathedral and near Robert's house on Southgate Street, the place where he also had the book printing and newspaper business which he had inherited from his father. Also, there were many chimney sweeps and other poor children in the area. Through school, they would be able to hear about God, learn to read, cultivate manners, and discover the importance of cleanliness.

Robert Raikes was a benevolent, kind-hearted man—a sort of pied piper. The children were drawn to him and to his school, eager to learn.

Once there, the children were encouraged to wash their faces and hands and comb their hair. Many had never seen a real comb before. Their hair was so thickly matted with grime that they could only comb it with their fingers. Right away they were taught:

> Clean hands, clean face, and tidy combed hair,
> Are better than fine clothes to wear.[1]

Raikes treated the children gently, but certain expectations needed to be met. If they came to school clean, he patted their heads or cheeks and told them how fine they looked. He gave them prizes for good behavior and cleanliness, a comb, a shilling, a book, even shoes if they had none, and other "encouragements."

Most of the children loved coming to school. A few who resisted were sometimes sent by their parents with weights tied to their ankles to keep them from running away.

Once Robert got the boys interested in school, he established classes for girls. When he thought they were becoming "civilized," he bought them each a nice bonnet to wear.

Besides reading, manners, and cleanliness, the children were taught the Scriptures and the catechism. Robert also devised a plan to help the boys and girls buy new clothes. When they had a penny to bring, he doubled it so they could purchase new clothing and save a little money besides.

Raikes regularly visited the children's homes to ask about their behavior and check on the conduct of the parents. While he visited with them, he admonished them to keep their houses clean and gave them hints about child-rearing. Some parents told him they could keep their children in line merely by saying that Mr. Raikes would hear about it if they did not behave.

Robert believed that it was easier for children to learn if they had the proper amount of food to eat. Since many of them came to school hungry, he often bought bread for his little scholars.

Robert's teaching was lively. One day he used a magnet to explain that an invisible power such as God could exist and draw people to himself. He then demonstrated that a magnetized needle could also draw objects to itself. "You, too," he told the children, "can be instruments of God and draw others to Christ."

Many of the boys and girls were so excited by learning that at work they kept books by their looms to read and study when threads broke and the machines needed rethreading.

On New Year's Day in 1795 Mr. Raikes invited all his Sunday school children to join him and his family to dine on roast beef and plum pudding. The children were clean and happy, and enthusiastically sang praises to God. Robert felt very proud of the children and pleased with all they were learning.

Although many people began to see the value of Sunday schools in "civilizing" what society called "the lower order of people," there were also violent objections to what Mr. Raikes was doing. A publication called the *Gentleman's Magazine* was a principal opponent. In one of the 1797 issues, a writer insisted that by educating the poor, society would make them "unfit for menial service, raise discontent, and foment rebellion." The article ended with, "We may, therefore, conclude that the Sunday school is so far from being the wise, useful, or prudential institution [it is said to be] that it is in reality productive of no valuable advantage, but, on the contrary, is subversive of that order, . . . [and] merits our contempt, and ought to be exploded as the vain chimerical institution of a visionary projector."[2]

Even those who supported Robert Raikes's work were afraid that teaching the common people would have far-reaching and dangerous consequences. They believed the masses would be content only as long as they were ignorant.

Serious opposition also came from Scotland. The Rev. Thomas Burns in 1798 thundered against Sunday schools from his pulpit in Renfrew. "I can see no necessity for the institution, and I am afraid men do not consider the effects that are likely to follow." He went on to say that perhaps such an institution was necessary in England where few parents were qualified to teach their children, but there could be no such argument for the parents in Scotland where every parish was provided with means of instruction. "Sunday schools, then," he concluded, "are reflections on every parish where they are appointed; nay, more, they are reflections upon every parent in that parish. It is declaring to the world that there is a parish where the parents are either grossly ignorant or shamefully negligent. . . . I repeat it again, my great objection to Sunday schools is that I am afraid they will in the end destroy all family religion, and whatever has tendency to do this I consider it is my duty to guard you against."[3]

Frequently Robert felt depressed and alone in his work. He wrote to a minister friend, the Rev. William Lewelyn of Leominster, ". . . I walk alone. It seems as if I had discovered a new country where no other adventurer chooses to follow."[4]

Another time he wrote, "Perhaps the depression of what is mortal may be necessary to elevate the immortal part of our nature. . . . I am never in so proper a frame of mind as whilst I am reading or repeating passages from that heavenly composition [the Psalms]. They are my chief comfort and consolation when any distress approaches; they furnish the language of thanksgiving when the heart rejoices."[5]

The work of the Sunday schools appeared to carry over into daily life. One day Mr. Raikes asked Mr. Church, a manufacturer of hemp and flax, if there was any change in the behavior of the children he employed. Mr. Church answered, "Sir, the change could not have been more extraordinary, in my opinion, had they been transformed from the shape of wolves and tigers to that of men. . . . Since the establishment of Sunday schools . . . they are also become more tractable and obedient, and less quarrelsome and revengeful. In short, I never conceived that a reformation so singular could have been effected amongst the set of untutored beings I employed."[6]

Many people saw "sin" as the behavior of criminals—the "lower orders" as the poor were often called. But not Raikes. Again he wrote to his friend, Mr. Lewelyn. "Your writings have strengthened and refreshed my drooping heart. I see my own unworthiness more clearly, and with this plea I go more boldly to the Throne of Mercy, . . . having faith and confidence in His power to restore. Without this hope of relief, the pressure of my sins would be a burden too heavy for me to bear.

"However, this is language which I speak only to you and to my own heart. The world would laugh. They conceive that notorious crimes are all that we have to guard against. But you and I have not so learned Christ!"[7]

Sunday school instruction soon spread to other areas. A school in one of these places invited Robert to a celebration to see the amazing change in the "young savages." The clean, though ragged children sat reverently during the entire service in full view of the congregation. Every child joined in the Lord's Prayer. After the service the children responded to questions. Some could read the New Testament and a few repeated whole chapters. Fifty of them recited hymns and the catechism perfectly.

One gentleman pointed to a ragged-looking lad of about thirteen and said to Raikes, "That boy was the most profligate little boy in this neighborhood. He was the leader of every kind of mischief and wickedness. He never opened his lips without a profane or indecent expression. And now he is become orderly and good natured, and, in his conversation, quite left off profaneness."[8]

The people in the parish of Painswick also changed from criticism to praise of the Sunday schools. Now they were able to attend worship and leave their houses and gardens without having them vandalized by mischief-makers.

The Sunday school affected the adults of Painswick as well. Each year they had an annual Sunday festival which was usually celebrated with drunk and disorderly conduct. This year, however, the community and neighboring villages were invited to come see a program by three hundred children from various schools, so the people came to church instead of going to the alehouse. The pews and aisles were packed. Everyone marveled at the change that produced such clean and orderly boys and girls, and no doubt they took a look at their own behavior. Even the very generous offering from a financially poor congregation indicated confidence in the Sunday school. A carpenter put in a guinea, then contributed four extra guineas in private lest he look ostentatious.

Finally, in 1788, the same *Gentleman's Magazine* that had once attacked Raikes so viciously reported on a meeting between Raikes and the Queen of England in which she praised his work. The magazine conceded that the accomplishments of Raikes were, indeed, commendable. In time, Sunday schools were springing up all over the world.

Historical consensus seems to place Robert Raikes as the founder of the national Sunday school movement, although certainly others instructed the young at various times and places. The Sunday school continues to be a vibrant place, making connections between faith and daily living.

Notes

1. J. Henry Harris, ed., *Robert Raikes, The Man and His Work* (New York: E. P. Dutton, n.d.), 23.

2. Ibid., 92.

3. Ibid., 96–98.

4. Ibid., 84.

5. Ibid., 96.

6. Ibid., 312.

7. Ibid., 197–98.

8. Ibid., 314.

12 *Elizabeth Fry*   1780–1845

The prison keeper marched into the governor's quarters. "Two women from the Society of Friends want to see you, sir. One is Elizabeth Fry. They want to be let into the women's section of the prison."

"What?" The governor wrinkled his nose. "Even I don't venture into the female section here at Newgate."

"Nor I," agreed the London prison guard. "That unruly mob would at the very least tear off my clothes. But these women are insistent."

The governor of Newgate Prison pondered a minute. "Well, I'll see them then."

As the keeper went to fetch the women, the governor heaved a deep sigh. The past two days had been disturbing. First there was that visit from a member of the Society of Friends, Stephen Grellet, who preached to the mobs on the streets. His preaching had a sobering effect on many. Afterwards he insisted on visiting the prisoners. He objected to the conditions he found and must have reported to Elizabeth Fry. The governor hadn't met Mrs. Fry yet, but he knew she was an effective leader and preacher for the Society of Friends and also active in helping the poor of the city.

Although the governor thought he had become quite hardened to weekly hangings at the prison, he was haunted by memories of yesterday's events. The carnival-like atmosphere yesterday unsettled him.

The day replayed in his mind. Workmen built a temporary scaffold late Sunday night or during the early morning hours. By 7:00 A.M. Monday the shouting, jeering mob began to gather, vying with each other for the best view. Some of the window seats overlooking the gallows went for ten pounds each. Then, as the prison funeral bell tolled, the young, female prisoner was brought out to be hanged for forging a bank note.

She looked so frightened as she was pushed toward the scaffold while people in the crowd roared and stamped their feet. Once the rope was secured around the prisoner's neck, the trap door was pulled away suddenly. As her body fell, the noose tightened about her neck. She struggled briefly, then went limp.

Afterwards, the governor gave a hanging breakfast for his friends. They chatted and joked and watched the body swing to and fro as they ate. When they had stuffed themselves, they went out to watch as the corpse was cut down. Somehow, reviewing the scene troubled the governor. It had never bothered him before. Didn't people get what they deserved?

Just then the guard returned with the two women. Their arms were full of flannel baby clothes which the Society of Friends had made just yesterday after hearing from Grellet about the appalling conditions in the prisons. The governor tried to dissuade the women from going inside, but there was no arguing with Mrs. Fry. She was gracious but persuasive as she insisted that they be let into the prison.

"At least leave your watch behind," the governor finally told her.

Elizabeth Fry had seen poverty and suffering, but she was unprepared for what she was about to see. As the door locked behind them, she and Anna faced about three hundred women crowded into two rooms. Children were hungry, cold, and crying. Many babies were naked and some were dying or already dead.

Sleeping space was arranged in tiers. The first layer of bodies lay on the floor and two other tiers hung in hammocks. Few prisoners had bedding. Young prisoners were housed with hardened crones. Some women were fighting, pulling hair, scratching at each other's eyes, yelling, and cursing. If they received money from begging at the barred windows, there was sure to be a fight over it. Some women were playing with filthy cards or reading literature which Mrs. Fry considered most unwholesome. There were no washing facilities and the smell of unclean bodies was overpowering. Everyone was hungry. Each prisoner was allowed only a crust of bread and a small amount of water daily.

Elizabeth and Anna set to work immediately, dressing all the babies in flannel clothes and comforting the mothers. They toured the upstairs where they discovered sick women lying on bare floor except for a bit of scattered straw. "Something must be done for these poor women," Elizabeth told Anna.

The next day Elizabeth and Anna returned to Newgate. They brought thick, clean straw for the sick women, more clothes for the babies, and a few other necessities. They said prayers with the women and talked to them about God. Although Elizabeth tended to speak in a condescending manner, the women were attracted to her dignity, her gentle ways, and musical voice.

Although her work at the prison was important to Elizabeth, she was unable to continue her work for four more years because of family matters. When she returned to the prison she was again overwhelmed by the horrible conditions. It was time for action.

As before, the prisoners were amazed to see the distinguished, Quaker woman coming to see them. "Why does she come into a place like this when she doesn't have to?" whispered one.

"Let's listen," answered a woman with long, stringy hair. "She's going to talk to us."

"Maybe she'll give us money," hissed a third through a mouth of missing teeth. "She looks like a person we can get something out of."

Curious, the forgers, prostitutes, thieves, and others gathered around Mrs. Fry. "We are each different, but we have many things in common. I am a mother too," Elizabeth told the women. "I have a large family and I'm still breast-feeding an eight-month-old baby." Immediately the women felt a connection with Mrs. Fry. "I worry about my children," she went on, "but I also worry about all children. It distresses me to see the children here in such bad circumstances." She motioned to the children. "Is there not something we can do for these innocent children? Can we help them so they do not become thieves or worse?"

The women were stunned. This visitor was asking *their* opinion. No one ever bothered to learn what they thought about anything. Instead, the public laughed and jeered at them, poked fun, and insulted them. The authorities treated them like nonpersons. Even the visiting chaplain, Dr. Cotton, did not talk to them as individuals. Some of the women began to weep because here was someone who showed love and concern for them.

As Elizabeth talked with the inmates, they began to see that a school was needed in the prison. Excitedly they promised to help in any way they could. Next Elizabeth had to convince the authorities.

She met with the governor of Newgate prison, two sheriffs of London, and the ordinary of the prison. As she explained her plan to the gentlemen, they listened politely. "A fine idea, Mrs. Fry," said one of the sheriffs, "but it will never work. You just do not understand the nature of the problem in our prisons."

"It's to your credit," added the governor, "that you want to uplift these women. But they are incorrigible."

"And vicious," added the ordinary. "Their children are too. They would steal all the supplies and turn the place into a roughhouse."

"I would at least like to try," said Mrs. Fry. "The women need something to do. Perhaps they will be less of a problem if they are kept busy."

"We do not have space enough," said the ordinary. "The prison is overcrowded now, although we have made improvements since you were here four years ago. There was pressure from the public after you brought conditions to their attention."

"Is it then space alone that prevents us from organizing a school?" asked Mrs. Fry innocently.

The men agreed. Yes, yes, of course, this was the most pressing problem.

Elizabeth went back to tell the women of her meeting with the authorities and the problem from their point of view. Together, with the women helping make the decision, it was decided that one of the smaller cells could be utilized as a schoolroom.

Elizabeth returned to the authorities. "We have a room for our school," she told them. Now the governor and sheriffs and ordinary were cornered. It was not easy to argue with this gentle, persuasive woman who was highly respected in the community and the wife of a prominent merchant as well. The men did tell Mrs. Fry, however, that her experiment would surely fail, but she must find out for herself.

The very next day Elizabeth started the school. From among the prisoners, she found someone to be the teacher—a young, educated woman who was in jail for stealing a watch. Most of the youngsters who began class that day had been born in prison and were under the age of seven. Some of them also were convicted of crimes.

Outside the schoolroom prisoners in their teens and twenties begged to go to class too. "We want to learn how to read and sew, and learn an occupation," they said. So Elizabeth recruited friends to help her organize classes for all who were interested.

At first Elizabeth's friends were intimidated by the women cursing, fighting, chewing and spitting tobacco, singing lewd songs, and carrying on in ways that were too embarrassing to discuss. They admired the calm, reassuring manner in which Elizabeth moved among the crowd. Her dignified and rather imperious manner inspired respect immediately as she sternly but lovingly ministered to the women.

Each day Elizabeth and her helpers brought baskets to the prison which contained Bibles, tracts, small articles of clothing, sewing materials, and sometimes dinners.

Next Elizabeth decided that as the prisoners developed useful skills, they could make things to sell. She needed help for such an ambitious project so she turned to her brothers-in-law. They gave her no support. Each one had a similar line: "The prisoners will steal all the materials. It's not practical. It will never work. In Newgate you have the scum of London, and they're beyond hope. Your school will be mocked."

There was no discouraging Elizabeth. Her prayer to God always had been that she might live in the fear of God rather than of human beings, and that neither good nor evil report from others would move her in the least.[1] With no help promised by the men, Elizabeth then turned to the women of the community and set up a committee called The Association for the Improvement of the Female Prisoners in Newgate. Committee members, some Quakers and some from other parts of the community, began visiting the prisoners daily. They agreed to pay the salary of a resident matron, to buy work materials for the women, and to arrange to sell items that they made. The committee also supplied the inmates with clothes and bedding, introduced them to the Holy Scriptures, and encouraged habits of order and sobriety. Not only would this help the women behave better in prison, but also make them respectable when they left.

The authorities, of course, were skeptical of the program. The governor finally agreed to come see for himself what effect such an approach was having on the inmates. He was quite astonished when he saw clean, orderly women learning new skills. He saw that they listened respectfully to Mrs. Fry as she read the story of the prodigal son from the Scriptures.

He was so impressed that he agreed to whitewash the walls and fix up the former laundry at Newgate so the women could have a workroom. Elizabeth arranged with a manufacturer to buy whatever items the prisoners produced, and Quaker merchants promised to furnish scrap materials free of charge. The prison improvement committee assured Elizabeth they would pay the women one shilling for every five they earned. Elizabeth was to keep track of the transactions and do her best to make the prisoners comfortable.

At a meeting with the inmates, Elizabeth explained that she and her helpers were not there to rule over them, but to work together with them to better their condition. Not a rule would be made without their unanimous consent. For those days, this was an astonishing idea.

Amazingly, the women agreed unanimously to be monitored by those within their own ranks, work with clean hands, gather to hear Scripture read each morning and evening, and act in an orderly manner.

Word soon spread about the new program in the women's prison. Visitors, including the Lord Mayor of London, sheriffs, and aldermen came to check out the rumors. They were astonished to see such a change in infamous Newgate Prison.

In time Elizabeth Fry's idea caught on and soon reforms sprang up all over England and in neighboring countries.

Although Elizabeth Fry was always in poor health, she seemed to be energized by social causes. All her life she was determined to make Christ's teachings her priority, and that included a concern for the suffering and needy. She had a large family but did not enjoy managing her disorganized and undisciplined household, so the children were frequently left to the care of relatives or hired help. She was criticized a great deal for traveling about the country preaching, reforming, and being busy with everything but her own family of eleven children. Her husband, however, admired her and supported her work. "I hope, if you should live to grow up," she wrote to her children when she was away on one of her trips, "you will endeavour to be very useful and not spend all your time in pleasing yourselves."[2]

When the Frys suffered financial difficulties, they lost many of their "friends" and their standing in the community. Some people, including the prison chaplain, Mr. Cotton, tried to discredit Elizabeth Fry's success. That led her to inspect prisons in other countries, and before long effective reforms began taking place in many locations.

Notes

1. June Rose, *Elizabeth Fry: A Biography* (New York: St. Martin's Press, 1980), 95.

2. Ibid., 71.

13 *Pasha Tichomirow*   b. 1888

The chill Siberian wind blew through the cracks of the gloomy orphanage barracks. The noise from three hundred boys crescendoed as they yelled, swore, and shoved while they performed their chores or played their games. "I've got to run away!" Pasha whispered to himself. "I can't stay another day in this awful place!"

Because Pasha was a new arrival, he was a natural target for teasing and cruel pranks. He missed his mother and father dreadfully, and now his older sister had been forcibly separated from him and sent to a different orphanage. He might never see her again!

Pasha waited until dark. Meanwhile he forced down another horrible supper of dried fish soup. A heavy-set bully knocked him in the ribs. Another grabbed his ration of dry, black bread and called him names. Pasha's determination to escape was stronger than ever, yet he knew the rules. "No one leaves the barracks unless accompanied." He must be careful.

During all the table-clearing commotion, Pasha saw his chance. He slipped out into the night, climbed over a low place in a wall of boards, and began to run. Fortunately there was no moon so darkness covered him as he raced across four miles of open fields. On and on he ran until his lungs felt as if they would burst. His legs ached, and his feet were blistered from his shoes.

Finally he reached the protection of the woods and could go no farther. He dropped to sleep in the hollow of a tree and began to dream that a big man was chasing him. His legs wouldn't move. The man caught him and carried him back to the barracks. Ugly faces lectured him and poured fish soup down his throat.

In the morning Pasha awoke to sunshine and melting snow. Birds were singing. He lay in the hollow, thinking. What should he do now? He had to eat, but above all, he wanted to return to his home village in Sosnowka. How far away was it? Hundreds of miles? Thousands? His family had traveled for months to come this far.

How happy life had been in Sosnowka. A beautiful river ran by his home where he swam and fished. He and his older sister, Shura, belonged to a loving family. Now all that had changed.

He remembered the day his father said, "We are moving to Siberia!" One bad harvest after another compelled a whole group of farmers to sell their farms and set out for Tomsk in Siberia where cheap land was available. The trip was slow. Trains made long stops along the way, and sometimes it took weeks to catch a train going toward Tomsk. The passengers had to sleep on the floor of the train stations. Hot food was a luxury they couldn't afford so they subsisted on dried fish and drank polluted water.

Soon cholera broke out. On the last stretch of the journey Mr. Tichomirow came down with the plague. He was removed from the train and put in a barracks for people with infectious diseases. Mrs. Tichomirow, eight-year-old Pasha, and Shura left the train, too, and waited as each day brought grim news about Mr. Tichomirow.

Then Mrs. Tichomirow came down with cholera and was carried away on a stretcher. Pasha and Shura ran behind, crying, until the heavy barracks door was slammed in their faces. That night they huddled behind a snow fence. Shura stayed awake all night to keep Pasha warm. The next day they went to the barracks many times until finally a guard snapped, "Do not come here again. Both your father and mother are dead."

"I don't want to live anymore," wailed Pasha. "I'm going to throw myself under the train!" Shura did her best to comfort her brother. God will not forsake us," she whispered.

In the morning the children set out for the next village to find food. Suddenly a coarse voice demanded, "What are you doing here?" Rough hands grabbed them and sent them sobbing to separate orphanages.

The shrill song of a bird brought Pasha back to the present. It would be a long journey back home, but he wanted to get as far away as possible from the hated orphanage barracks. He set out cautiously, careful to avoid the main roads where someone might be searching for a runaway boy.

After a second night under a tree, Pasha was awakened by loud voices. Someone slapped him on the back. "Hey there, young fellow! Who are you? What are you doing here in the chill dawn?"

Pasha looked with terror into the faces of three rough-looking armed men. He knew at once that they were not from the barracks, so he told them his tale. "You are a clever lad," said one of the men. "We invite you to come with us. You will have food and a warm fire at night, and you won't be alone. We'll make something of you!"

Pasha didn't dare refuse an offer from armed men. One of them hoisted him onto a horse in front of him and off they galloped through the tangled forest and along winding trails until they came to a clearing where about twenty men and women were gathered. All of them stared at Pasha. "Where did you get *him*?" one woman asked, staring at Pasha's dirty clothes and body. "What's your family name?"

"Tichomirow," answered Pasha. "It means 'quiet peace.' "

"That name does not fit with us," answered a jovial man. "We will call you 'Greasy,' because that's what you are. Dirty and greasy."

Suddenly Pasha realized that he was in a robber's den! But it didn't take him long to become acquainted with his new life. There was good food, jolly company, and freedom from drudgery. Soon he forgot all about his plans to return to Sosnowka. It was comforting to be among friendly people and fun to see all the loot that they brought back each day from their forays into surrounding villages.

Greasy soon became the pet of the robber band. He was clever, intelligent, and quick, and his superiors taught him well. In no time he was stealing right along with the rest. Now and then he remembered what he had once been taught about the sin of stealing, but he managed to drive such thoughts back into his subconscious.

Eight years passed, and Greasy was now sixteen years old. He had become assistant to the leader of the gang, and together they preyed on villages for seventy-five miles around. No one could find them in the deep woods which were surrounded by thickets and dense vegetation.

One day when they were out pillaging, the band split in two, and Greasy was put in charge of one group. His party came upon two men who were traveling through the woods. The bandits threatened the travelers, but the men dropped to their knees and begged, "Please spare our lives! We will give you everything we have!" Greasy's robbers ignored their pleas and murdered them both, then took their clothing, boots, rubles and kopeken, a sack of utensils, and two books.

"Let's throw away the books, Greasy," said a comrade. "They're just worthless junk."

"We'll keep them," ordered Greasy. "They might be useful for cigarette papers." He put the books among his things.

That night before going to sleep, Greasy pulled out the books. One was entitled *The Voice of Faith*, and the other, *The New Testament*. As he lay in his bunk, he idly leafed through the Testament and came upon a passage in Romans 3:11-18. "There is no one who seeks God. . . . Their throats are opened graves; they use their tongues to deceive. . . . Their mouths are full of cursing and bitterness. Their feet are swift to shed blood; ruin and misery are in their paths, and the way of peace they have not known. There is no fear of God before their eyes." The startling words brought back a picture—the murdered victims pleading for their lives.

Who were these men? he wondered. He spotted an inscription on the flyleaf of the New Testament. "May 15, 1898, the day of conversion to the Lord, my repentance and new birth. On this day He forgave my sins and washed me with His holy blood."[1]

Greasy didn't understand the words, so began turning more pages. "Do you not know that wrongdoers will not inherit the kingdom of God?" He read the list of evil deeds with the final summary, "And this is what some of you used to be. But you were washed, you were sanctified, you were justified in the name of the Lord Jesus Christ and in the Spirit of our God" (1 Cor. 6:9-11).

Next Greasy came upon the story of Zacchaeus who was so changed by the love and power of God that he promised to give back four times what he had stolen as well as half of all his other goods. Greasy kept turning pages. There was the story of the crucifixion. He read about the repentant thief and Jesus' promise of paradise.

The young robber was deeply troubled. He shut the book and put it under his pillow. That thief was forgiven! God's love seemed to have no limits. Again the scene of the pleading victims tormented his mind. All night he tossed. In the morning the others asked, "What's wrong with you?" Finally Greasy said, "I am no longer at peace with what we are doing. The book we stole has a strange power over me."

"Let's burn that book!" said one robber. "It's witchcraft!"

"Let's not burn it," said another, "but see for ourselves what is in it." Greasy began to read aloud while the robbers listened. One of the young men said, "I recognize that book. It's a New Testament. My mother was a *Stundist*—a believer. She used to take me to meetings where we read this book, and sang and prayed."

Day after day Greasy read from the Bible. Its powerful words created a restlessness among the men and women and dulled the exhilaration they had always felt when they went plundering.

A month passed. Daily the robbers continued to listen as Greasy read from the New Testament. Finally the robber whose mother was a believer said, "I cannot take part in this kind of life. I am going to turn myself in to the authorities."

"I will turn myself in too," said Greasy. Six others declared they would do the same. The day of parting came. Once more Greasy read from the remarkable book. Afterwards he fell on his knees and confessed his sins before God. Others followed, and weeping filled the air as they begged a holy God for forgiveness. Finally the good friends said their farewells.

Greasy and his six friends went to the city. When people saw the armed group in their colorful dress, they stared. "Who are those men?" they asked. "What are they doing in our city?"

The robbers went to the office of Jurij Nikolajewitch, the state attorney of the district court. They laid down their weapons and told their story. "We will take whatever punishment we deserve," they added. Jurij was dumbfounded! What should he do with men like these? As he prepared to write up his report, young Greasy told him, "I would no longer be called Greasy, but Paul Tichomirow, and I will hereafter serve God and mankind, and without murmuring take upon myself the punishment determined by the law. We are now in your hands."[2] All his comrades made similar declarations.

The men were jailed separately, and that night Nikolajewitch said to his wife, "What do you think, Tanja? Do you think we should read the New Testament too, and see what power is in it that has changed these men?"

"I have already read it," answered Tatjana Alxandrowna. "Yet I cannot understand how the book could change the robbers so drastically."

Jurij went into his library and found a New Testament. He began to read. Dread came over him as he tackled the twelfth chapter of John. "The one who rejects me and does not receive my word has a judge; on the last day the word that I have spoken will serve as judge" (John 12:48). That night Jurij couldn't sleep. He wondered about this God who could change even robbers.

The next day the judges examined the prisoners. They, too, were puzzled by the authority of the book. Some of the judges decided to read it for themselves. When the town priest got wind of the story, he grew angry. "Paul Tichomirow and his comrades are stirring up the other prisoners," he railed. The whole town joined in and took up the argument. Some sided with the priest. Others were awed by the robbers' account.

After a year in jail, Paul and his comrades stood before the judgment bar. The authorities were astonished as they heard again the prisoners' confession and their willingness to take the consequences. Finally each man was sentenced to ten years hard labor.

Pasha, or Paul, was sent to the district beyond the Baikal Sea and the other prisoners were assigned to various other locations. Far and wide they told their stories, to their guards, to the courts, to the district authorities, to whomever would listen. As Paul labored in prison, the guards noticed the positive effect he was having on even the most unruly convicts.

Finally on a day of national celebration, amnesty was granted to many prisoners, including Pasha and his comrades. Paul set out to become an evangelist. From the time of his conversion, he had tried through letters and inquiries to learn of his sister, but so far nothing had come of his search. As he traveled and preached throughout the country, he found lodging with believers. In one town he stayed at the home of Allexej Wassiljewitch and was stunned to discover that the wife and mother in this Christian family was his own sister, Shura.

After a joyful reunion, Paul continued his witness throughout Russia. He was imprisoned many times for his faith, yet Christ lived through him with such strength and beauty that he inspired people wherever he went. On the flyleaf of the New Testament that he had taken from his murdered victim, he wrote his own inscription underneath the first. "Forgive me, for Christ's sake, beloved brother; I put you to death while I myself was dead in my sins. The Lord hath forgiven me and raised me to a new life. Thy untimely, bodily death was the means of leading not only me, but also many other sinners and murderers to the Eternal Life. Thy New Testament softened my hard heart as a living stream, stilled my thirst, and continues to flow farther, quickening and giving life to other souls also. For this I praise thy and my God. Amen."[3]

Notes

1. Chas. Lukesh, *"Greasy," The Robber* (Minneapolis: Osterhus Publishing Company, 1942), 13.

2. Ibid., 17.

3. Ibid., 31.

14 Corrie ten Boom 1892–1983
Betsie ten Boom 1885–1944

A cold September rain fell on hundreds of poorly clad women as they stood waiting for the 4:30 A.M. roll call. Dull gray buildings and towering concrete walls topped by barbed wire were barely visible in the gloom. As these new arrivals stood at attention, they couldn't shut out the dreadful sounds of anguish that came from the punishment barracks, a reminder to all who might consider being uncooperative at Ravensbruck Concentration Camp.

Corrie stood in line with her sister Betsie, and her mind could hardly comprehend the past eight months. Before their arrest, she and Betsie had been at Beje, the old family home in Haarlem, Holland, which also housed the ten Boom watch and clock repair shop. But ominous events had begun to change their world forever.

The ten Boom family became involved in the resistance movement and had been hiding Jews in their home. With the Nazis occupying Holland, their work became more and more precarious. Corrie remembered the night she, Betsie, and their father prayed long after the others had gone to bed. Should they stop their "subversive work"? No, they decided. "We knew that in spite of daily mounting risks we had no choice but to move forward," she said later. "This was evil's hour; we could not run away from it. Perhaps only when human effort had done its best and failed, would God's power alone be free to work."[1]

Corrie, Betsie, their aged father, and others in the family were finally arrested by the Nazis in February of 1944 and brought to the prison at Scheveningen, the Nazi headquarters in Holland. The chief interrogator considered letting eighty-four-year-old Mr. ten Boom go free, if he promised to cause no more trouble.

Mr. ten Boom stood erect, white hair crowning his aged frame. "If I go home today, tomorrow I will open my door again to anyone in need who knocks."[2] The old man died in prison shortly afterwards.

Betsie's coughing brought Corrie back to the present situation. "Dear God," Corrie thought, "Betsie mustn't die. We need her unselfish love, especially here."

After endless waiting for roll call and again for a crust of black bread, all newcomers were commanded to turn in their possessions, then march naked past the inspection line. Corrie knew how much they needed their forbidden Bible, also the one sweater for Betsie, and the bottle of vitamin drops. How could she hide these things?

Impulsively she asked a guard, "Where are the toilets?" He pointed to the shower room. "Use the drainholes," he growled. The sisters hurried to the deserted room. Benches covered with mildew and cockroaches were stacked in the corner. Quickly Corrie wrapped the Bible and vitamin bottle in the blue sweater and pushed it behind the benches. Following inspection, the lice-encrusted women were herded into icy showers.

As the prisoners pulled on their thin, regulation dresses, Corrie tied the sweater underneath hers, around her waist. Then she took the canvas bag that held the compact Bible, hung the attached string around her neck, and shoved it into her dress. "It made a bulge you could have seen across the Grote Markt," Corrie said later. "I flattened it out as best I could, pushing it down, tugging the sweater around my waist, but there was no real concealing it beneath the thin cotton dress. And all the while I had the incredible feeling that it didn't matter, that this was not my business, but God's. That all I had to do was walk straight ahead."[3] In line, guards ran their hands over every prisoner. When they came to Corrie, they let her pass, although the woman ahead of her was searched three times.

A second inspection line was supervised by female guards. As Corrie came through the line, a guard shoved her roughly and barked, "Move along! You're holding up the line." Betsie and Corrie arrived at their barracks with new faith in the power of God.

Each day life grew more insufferable, yet ". . . our Bible," said Corrie, "was the center of an ever-widening circle of help and hope.

Like waifs clustered around a blazing fire, we gathered about it, holding out our hearts to its warmth and light. The blacker the night around us grew, the brighter and truer and more beautiful burned the word of God. 'Who shall separate us from the love of Christ? Shall tribulation, or distress, or persecution, or famine, or nakedness, or peril, or sword?' "[4]

"I would look about us as Betsie read," said Corrie, "watching the light leap from face to face. 'We are more than conquerors.' Life at Ravensbruck took place on two separate levels, mutually impossible. One, the observable, external life, grew every day more horrible. The other, the life we lived with God, grew daily better, truth upon truth, glory upon glory."[5]

Betsie was now coughing constantly. Corrie doled out a few drops of the vitamins for her each morning on her black bread. "I wonder how much longer this bottle can last," she told Betsie. "Especially when you keep sharing it around every time someone sneezes."[6]

As new prisoners swarmed into Ravensbruck, Betsie and Corrie were moved to Barracks 28, an enormous building with a knitting room in the center and huge sleeping rooms on either side. The place was built to sleep 400, but 1,400 prisoners from every country were crammed together. Instead of beds, there were straw-covered platforms stacked three high all up and down the barracks, with narrow aisles between. Too few toilets stank and overflowed. Rags were poked into broken windows. As the women crawled into their filthy, reeking platforms, they suddenly discovered the entire area was swarming with fleas. "Betsie," shrieked Corrie. "How can we live in such a place?"

Betsie was already praying, "Show us, Lord, how to give thanks in all circumstances." They were thankful that they were together, and that they had their Bible, but the fleas! How could they give thanks for the fleas?

"All circumstances," Betsie reminded Corrie, but Corrie was sure this time Betsie was wrong.

When lights went out that night, Corrie couldn't sleep. She thought of the female guard who struck Betsie across the mouth that afternoon, as well as the cruelty from hardened female guards at Vught, the camp before Ravensbruck. She remembered Betsie's words. "These young women, Corrie . . . if people can be taught to hate, they can be taught to love! We must find the way, you and I, no matter how long it takes."[7] Betsie saw a wounded human being in every cruel person. It was harder for Corrie, who trudged the "all-too-solid earth."

As Corrie watched the searchlights sweep the sky, her mind went back to an incident at Vught. In the factory she heard about Jan Vogel, one of her own countrymen. She discovered that he was the one who betrayed the ten Booms and other resistance workers. The news caused such intense hatred to well up in Corrie that she developed headaches, lost sleep, and couldn't concentrate at work. "Betsie," Corrie asked in exasperation one night. "Doesn't it bother you that Jan is the one who informed on us?"

"Oh yes, Corrie! Terribly!" answered Betsie. "I've felt for him ever since I knew—and pray for him whenever his name comes into my mind. How dreadfully he must be suffering!"[8]

Corrie remembered thinking that this sister of hers somehow belonged to another order of beings. "Wasn't she telling me in her gentle way that I was as guilty as Jan Vogel?" Corrie wondered. "Didn't he and I stand together before an all-seeing God convicted of the same sin of murder? For I had murdered him with my heart and with my tongue."[9] That night Corrie forgave her enemy and prayed for him, too, then slept for the first time in a week.

As she reviewed these episodes, Corrie realized all that Betsie was teaching her. As the days went by, fights broke out frequently among the nationality groups in Barracks 28. Betsie prayed for peace and gradually her example brought changes throughout the crowded quarters: thank yous, apologies, compromises, and bits of humor in place of snarls and insults.

The two sisters cautiously held Bible studies and prayer meetings in the barracks with various women translating, and soon the meetings grew until a second service was organized. Strangely enough, the guards never came near Barracks 28. In other places they marched back and forth, keeping close watch on every activity of the prisoners. By chance, Betsie found out why they stayed away. The guards were avoiding the fleas!

Another unusual occurrence concerned the bottle of vitamin drops. Betsie kept sharing it, much to Corrie's dismay, but it never ran out. Corrie wanted to hoard it because Betsie was growing weaker, yet she could never see how much was left in the dark, glass bottle. When a Dutch woman was assigned to the hospital, she smuggled a bottle of vitamins and some yeast compound into Barracks 28, and that day Corrie could not squeeze out even one more drop from the old bottle.

Under Betsie's prodding, Corrie and the other women began to pray daily for the brutal guards, for other prisoners, and for the healing of Germany. As Betsie grew weaker, she developed a clear sense of what God wanted from them after the war. There must be a house in Holland where all who had been hurt by hate could come for healing. "It's such a beautiful house, Corrie! The floors are all inlaid wood, with statues set in the walls and a broad staircase sweeping down. And gardens! . . . It will do them such good, Corrie, to care for flowers!"[10]

As the bitter winter grew more intense, everyone's suffering increased, and so did Corrie's selfishness, which she justified, "for Betsie's sake." She maneuvered their way toward the middle of roll-call formation so they would be protected from the wind. After all, the Polish women wouldn't feel the cold as much as they did because it was colder in Poland. Because of their own special ministry, it was important for them to keep well. The yeast compound must last for Betsie's sake, so Corrie began taking it out after lights were out. "It isn't wrong, God, is it? It's nothing compared to the evil I see every day."

The selfishness, like a cancer, spread. In December every prisoner was given an extra blanket, but when new refugees arrived from Czechoslovakia, a woman assigned to Corrie's platform had no blanket at all. Betsie told Corrie they must give up one of theirs. Corrie lent the blanket, but did not give it. In her heart she held onto that blanket.

Somehow the joy and power began to drain from their ministry. Was it because of the selfishness, or was it coincidence? Corrie's prayers became mechanical, and Bible reading dull and lifeless. Betsie tried to take over for Corrie, but her cough was so bad that she couldn't read or pray aloud.

One night as Corrie read about the apostle Paul's thorn in the flesh, she suddenly realized that her selfishness was her thorn in the flesh. She closed her Bible and confessed her stinginess and lack of love to the women gathered there. And that night real joy returned to the worship.

One morning Betsie could not rise from her bed. Her life continued to ebb until she whispered her last instructions to Corrie from a stretcher at the hospital. "[We] must tell people what we have learned here. We must tell them that there is no pit so deep that He is not deeper still. They must listen to us, Corrie, because we have been here. . . . By the first of the year, Corrie, we will be out of prison!"[11]

Corrie was forced back to work, and when she next saw Betsie, she could hardly believe her eyes. Lying along a wall with all the other corpses, Betsie's eyes were closed as if in peaceful sleep. Her face looked young, full, and radiant. The hollow cheeks and the lines of grief and suffering were gone! "This is the Betsie of heaven," Corrie whispered, "released to heaven." A short time later Corrie, too, was released— released from prison—both before new year's, just as Betsie had said. Many years later Corrie learned that her release had been the result of a "clerical error"; one week later all the women her age were exterminated in the gas chambers.

After recovering from prison abuse, Corrie remembered, "We must tell them, Corrie, about what we experienced here." She began to speak about how God could work even under the worst circumstances. She talked of Betsie's vision of a home for war-damaged people.

A wealthy widow, Mrs. Bierens de Haan offered her splendid fifty-six-room mansion in Bloemendaal for the work. When Corrie saw the place, she was awed. It had inlaid floors, statues set along the walls, a broad staircase, and gardens all around. It became a place of healing and new beginnings.

Reluctantly Corrie began speaking in Germany too. At the close of a church service in Munich, she saw a man making his way to the front. An S.S. guard from Ravensbruck! Hate flooded Corrie's heart. All the words she had preached about forgiveness suddenly seemed hollow.

The former guard confessed to Corrie how grateful he was for her message of forgiveness. Then he put out his hand to her. She tried to smile and raise her hand, but could not. How could she forgive this man? Yet, didn't Christ die for him too? She must obey. "Forgive me, Lord, Jesus," she prayed silently. "I cannot forgive him. Give me your forgiveness."

She took his hand, and suddenly it happened. "From my shoulder along my arm and through my hand a current seemed to pass from me to him, while into my heart sprang a love for this stranger that almost overwhelmed me.

"And so I discovered that it is not on our forgiveness any more than on our goodness that the world's healing hinges, but on His. When He tells us to love our enemies, He gives, along with the command, the love itself."[12]

Another surprise came when Corrie was asked to help open a rehabilitation center at a former concentration camp in Darmstadt, Germany. With wonder, she remembered that just before her death, Betsie had described such a camp, a place of healing for the German people. As Corrie surveyed the drab barracks she announced, "Windowboxes. We'll have them at every window. The barbed wire must come down, of course, and then we'll need paint. Green paint. Bright yellow-green, the color of things coming up new in the spring,"[13] just as Betsie had planned.

Notes

1.   Corrie ten Boom with John and Elizabeth Sherrill, *The Hiding Place* (Minneapolis: World Wide Publications, 1971), 134.
2.   Ibid., 146.
3.   Ibid., 194.
4.   Ibid., 195.
5.   Ibid., 196.
6.   Ibid., 197.
7.   Ibid., 179.
8.   Ibid., 183.
9.   Ibid., 183.
10.   Ibid., 210.
11.   Ibid., 215.
12.   Ibid., 233.
13.   Ibid., 234.

15 *George Washington Carver*

1864–1943

George Washington Carver leaned back on his seat as the train chuffed along the tracks. He was on his way to Montgomery, Alabama, to speak at the United Peanut Association. He wondered what kind of reception he would receive this time.

Even though he was becoming a world-renowned scientist, Professor Carver knew that because he was black, he was not allowed many of the privileges of white people. Just a few moments ago he was concentrating on his talk and forgot that he had crossed the Mason-Dixon line into the South. "Move, nigger," the conductor reminded him. "You don't belong in the white car."

Speaking engagements were becoming a problem, because, although Professor Carver had countless invitations, many places did not accommodate black people. In some locations he could not enter a hotel or hospital by the front door, ride on the passenger elevators, shake hands with white people, drink from common fountains, or sleep in the same hotels.

Professor Carver closed his eyes, lulled by the clickety-clack of the wheels on the tracks. Silently he thanked his Creator for his gifts. He prayed, as he did each day, that he would use these gifts to bless all people, black and white, rich and poor alike. Especially though, he wanted to give hope and help to the people of his race who still struggled under prejudice, poverty, and educational disadvantages.

He was thankful, too, for all those who had helped him along the way, especially the Carvers, people who had nurtured his early start and treated him like a son. Childhood memories and the stories told to him tumbled through his mind. He was just a frail baby with whooping cough that terrifying night when slave raiders stole him and his mother. She was sent off to a new owner and never could be traced. Sickly George was easily traded back for a fine racing horse.

Although many blacks were not permitted to learn to read, the Carvers lived in Missouri which was not subject to such a law. George wanted to read more than anything, but the local school was for whites only. George begged God to help him find a way.

One day Mrs. Carver found an old primer in an attic trunk and gave it to him. To George this was more precious than gold, and he learned so fast that soon people all over the neighborhood were loaning him books. Already they called him Plant Doctor because he was so clever with growing things. He even made house calls to treat sick plants and flowers.

When George was only ten years old, he knew what he must do if he wanted an education. He left the only home he knew and set out with his small bundle of clothes. As he struggled through years of loneliness, prejudice, and many heartaches to get his education, God gave him courage. He finally graduated with honors and two degrees from Iowa State College in Ames. He loved teaching at the college there, but when Booker T. Washington, the highly respected president of Tuskegee Institute in Alabama asked him to come there, he couldn't refuse. This was where he could help his people the most.

Not only did he leave good friends at Iowa State, but a fine laboratory as well. Tuskegee had no lab and no money. The first thing Professor Carver did was to send his students out to knock on every door in town and ask for castaways: pots, pans, jars, old lamps, containers, odd dishes, bowls, cans, and jugs. Next they were instructed to go into the trash heaps and pull out junk that they washed and brought to the lab. The professor showed his classes how to convert the junk into useful equipment for their experiments.

George Carver remembered the early skepticism as he taught crop rotation, the composting of organic matter, and the recycling of everything imaginable. But in his mind, weren't Christians supposed to be good stewards of earth's resources and not waste any of God's gifts?

George smiled as he remembered the bug incident. He had the reputation for being able to identify any plant or insect. One day his students ingeniously fashioned a bug from parts of an ant, beetle, spider, and moth, and brought it to him to identify. He studied it, then with a twinkle said, "This, I think, is what we call a humbug."

The train was slowing. "Montgomery!" called the conductor. Professor Carver climbed down from the car, carrying his heavy specimen cases which were filled with peanut extracts.

When he reached the hotel where he was to speak, the doorman blocked his way. "What are you doing here, nigger?" he demanded.

"I am here to speak to the United Peanut Association," the professor replied politely.

The doorman looked dubiously at the black man in the baggy suit. "Yeah, sure. Well, they're meeting over at City Hall."

In sweltering temperatures George carried his heavy cases over to City Hall, only to get the runaround. He was finally sent back to the hotel. "I told you, no niggers allowed here," barked the doorman. "Get a move on!"

Professor Carver hastily scribbled a note to the president of the Peanut Association and asked a bellhop to deliver it. Finally he was ushered up the freight elevator and into the meeting. Many hostile faces greeted the black man in his well-worn suit. Little did they know that Mr. Carver repeatedly refused offers of new suits because he never discarded clothes with good wear left in them.

After he was introduced, Professor Carver calmly unpacked each product that he had developed from peanuts. As he talked, he wove witty remarks and humorous stories into his presentation. Tension eased as the listeners began laughing. Carver showed them breakfast food, shoe polish, vanishing cream, bleaching fluid, livestock meal, peanut milk, cheese, candies, linoleum, ink, and paper, all from the common peanut. Next came stains and dyes from peanut skins and tinware polish from ground-up hulls. Professor Carver explained that he had discovered more than three hundred products that could be made from peanuts, and from the sweet potato he had developed more than a hundred commodities. The peanut growers were astounded. Was it possible that a black man who was once a slave could be so smart? When Professor Carver finished speaking, the applauding crowd swarmed about him and promised to help him secure patents on his products.

In January George Washington Carver was asked by the Peanut Association to give a demonstration in Washington, D.C., to the Ways and Means Committee of the House of Representatives. Congress was writing a new tariff bill to protect the American farmer. Already there was a tax on imported meat, butter, and cheese. It was hoped that this scientist could create an interest in peanuts.

Professor Carver carried his samples into the place where the hearings were in progress. All afternoon he listened to debates, discussions, disagreements, statistics, and lists of figures as pecans, walnuts, and other items for the General Tariff Revision were considered and reconsidered. He could not believe the manner in which committee members spoke to each other with insults, accusations, and name-calling. Professor Carver always believed in speaking politely to others, even when disagreeing with them. "Do I have to speak to a group like this?" he asked himself.

It was nearly 4:00 and time for the meeting to end. "Professor George Washington Carver is to be our next speaker," announced Chairman Joseph W. Fordney. By now the committee members were bored, tired, and scrappy. Some of them looked askance at the black man in his old suit.

As Mr. Carver walked forward one congressman called out, "I suppose if you have plenty of peanuts and watermelons you're perfectly happy?"[1]

Another congressman from the South, smoking a cigar, was leaning back in his chair, had his feet on the table, and wore a hat pulled low on his face. "I suggest that you remove your hat during this meeting," requested Chairman Fordney.

Icily the southern congressman replied, "Down where I come from we don't accept any 'nigger's' testimony, and I don't see what this fellow can say that will have any bearing on this meeting."[2]

Professor Carver ignored the remarks. He tried never to let himself sink to the level of his tormentors. As he stepped up to the platform, the chairman announced, "Professor Carver, your time has been cut to ten minutes."

Carver knew he could never unpack his items in that amount of time. Nevertheless, he set out his specimens one by one, and as he talked about his products he injected his usual humor. His listeners warmed to him quickly. He had barely begun when the ten minutes were up. Congressman John N. Garner declared, "I think we should extend Professor Carver's time." The chairman and several other members agreed, so Professor Carver continued talking. Soon the southerner with the hat took the cigar from his mouth. Next he took his feet off the table. Finally he removed his hat.

Another congressman finally jumped up and said, "I vote that we give unlimited time to Mr. Carver." The approval was unanimous. Professor Carver displayed one amazing product after another, milks, oils, cheese, sauces, face cream, relish, mock meat and oysters, bleaching fluid, meal cake for livestock, ice cream powder, and many others. He talked for one hour and forty-five minutes! When he finished, the congressmen all rose to their feet and applauded.

Carver's demonstration resulted in the highest tariff ever for the peanut industry, a great boon to the agriculturally struggling South.

"God moves in a mysterious way, his wonders to perform," Mr. Carver said of the experience. "No matter what the circumstances, hatred and resentment must never have a place in our hearts."[3]

By commercializing his discoveries, George Washington Carver could have become a rich man, but with his frugal style of living, he did not need much money. He was more interested in having people of all classes and colors benefit from the products he developed. Although he did not crave glory for himself, he wanted credit for his race through him.

At Tuskegee, Professor Carver began a movable school on wheels so he could take his knowledge out to the farms. At country meetings he taught the farmers how to make their soil and seed most productive. He showed householders how to cook, clean, make curtains from flour sacks, rugs from corn shucks and grasses, and how to add beauty to their impoverished homes and yards. Carver did not permit people to wait on him because then, he said, he would not learn to do these things himself.

He encouraged families to raise food over and above what they needed so they could sell for profit and begin their long climb out of debt. "A good garden is one of the best family physicians," he said. "Have a garden, a little place by the house, even if it is only big enough to throw a dipper over it. But if you cannot afford to put a fence around, don't have it where the chickens can get in. And if a hen does make trouble and you want to throw something at her, throw shelled corn. The laborer is worthy of her hire, and she is entitled to half of what she earns."[4] Professor Carver insisted on treating livestock tenderly and providing good ventilation for animals going to market.

He helped white farmers as well as black because he said that one who did not answer the plea of others killed them in one's heart.

Professor Carver found that studying the Bible was a delight. "One must be entirely empty of self to hear the voice of the Lord,"[5] he said. At Tuskegee he had an optional Bible class. A religion teacher complained to the principal. "Professor Carver's teaching of the Bible is not in accord with orthodox theology."

"Is the class optional?" asked the principal.

"Well, yes, it is."

"Do many students attend?"

"Yes, the class is always overflowing."

"How long has this class been running?" the principal continued.

"Three years," answered the complainer.

The principal answered, "If anyone can have an optional Bible class for three years which is always crowded with eager students, no one had better interfere with such success."

Carver had a personal relationship with his Creator. He asked God's advice on everything he did. He arose at 4:00 each morning and spent time alone in prayer and meditation in the woods. He said, "Alone there with the things I love most, I gather my specimens and study the lessons Nature is so eager to teach us all. . . . At no other time have I so sharp an understanding of what God means to do with me as in these hours of dawn. . . ."[6]

"After I have had my morning talk with God, I go to my laboratory and begin to carry out his wishes for the day.[7] I never have to grope for methods; the method is revealed at the moment I am inspired to create something new. Without God to draw aside the curtain I would be helpless."[8]

Carver loved the words in Psalm 121, "I lift up mine eyes unto the hills—from where will my help come? My help comes from the LORD, who made heaven and earth." About this text he explained, "Now that doesn't mean just to look at the hills without seeing anything. It means to search. I take it to mean that I should try to see with every method at my command, with chemistry, with physics, as well as with my eyes. And by so doing, the help comes."[9]

Although blacks could not worship in white churches, white visitors were always welcome at the Tuskegee chapel. Once some ministers asked Carver what they could do to better race relations. He answered, "Your actions speak so loud I cannot hear what you are saying. You have too much religion and not enough Christianity—too many creeds and not enough performance. The world is perishing for kindness."[10]

This humble man died with a trail of honors and distinguished awards behind him, yet he once said of his relationship with God, "I would be able to do more if I were to stay in closer touch with him."[11]

Notes

1. Harvey Jay Hill, *"He Heard God's Whisper"* A Story of Dr. Geo. W. *Carver* (Minneapolis: Jorgenson Press, 1943), 74.

2. Rackham Holt, *George Washington Carver, An American Biography* (Garden City: Doubleday, Doran and Company, Inc., 1944), 177.
3. Ibid., 36.
4. Holt, *Biography*, 181.
5. Hill, *Whisper*, 36.
6. Holt, *Biography*, 265.
7. Ibid, 181–182.
8. Ibid., 282.
9. Ibid., 220.
10. Ibid., 282.
11. Ibid., 220.

16 *Dorothy Day* 1897–1980

Dorothy felt a tangle of emotions as she picked up her mail in the village and set off for home. As she hiked along she pondered the events of her life. Why had so many beginnings not worked out for her? A nurse's career, several unhappy love affairs, a painful, short-lived marriage. On top of it all the present relationship with her common-law husband, Forster, was becoming shaky; this was because she was developing an interest in religion.

It hadn't been so long ago that she had seldom given God a thought. At that time she had been involved with Communists, radicals, and anarchists, lived a nonconformist lifestyle and hung out in bars. She earned her living as a freelance writer for several left-wing papers. Yet, in spite of her apathy toward religion, the name of God still touched something deep within her.

The sound of birds calling to their mates from the treetops broke into Dorothy's thoughts and roused her senses. She felt the breeze, inhaled the fresh air, and noticed the flowers growing along the road. Such tender loveliness! She began to pray, a practice that was becoming more natural all the time. "With all this beauty around me, I cannot help but cry out in praise to God,"[1] she said.

Yet this joy was tinged with discouragement as she thought of all the quarrels she had with Forster lately over religion. He had brought such joy to her life. City-bred Dorothy was discovering a whole new world with Forster as he shared his love of nature with her. Together they hiked, collected beach specimens, studied the stars, and fished in the bay.

These activities only increased her wonder at God's handiwork. She began to read the Bible and pray. But when she talked to Forster about religion, immediately a wall separated them. He was an anarchist and an atheist and refused to discuss matters of faith. Yet he had introduced her to so many things that were good and beautiful, and this led her naturally to an interest in things of the spirit.

She remembered the experience of planting seeds in the garden. "I *must* believe in these seeds," she had said, "that they fall into the earth and grow into flowers and radishes and beans. It is a miracle to me because I do not understand it. Neither do naturalists understand it. The very fact that they use glib technical phrases does not make it any less of a miracle, and a miracle we all accept. Then why not accept God's mysteries?"[2]

As Dorothy walked, her mind continued to wander, mingling with her prayers. Her budding faith was swayed by the words of Jesus admonishing his followers to care for the unfortunate. She wished she knew more Christians whose personal morality was matched by a social morality. She felt angry because there were so many groups willing to *study* the problems of poverty and injustice, but too few willing to *do* anything about these problems. On all sides she saw people who had no provision for their basic needs, those disabled by war and unsafe factory conditions, or those who were victims of prejudice, ignorance, malnutrition, and exploitation. "Where are the saints," she asked, "who are willing to try to change the social order, not just minister to the slaves, but to do away with slavery?"[3]

Dorothy was discouraged with her own spiritual growth as well. She longed for a sense of wholeness and holiness, of transcendence, order, and obedience. She thought of her own willful personality. "I have reached the point," she said, "where I want to obey. . . . I am tired of following the devices and desires of my own heart, of doing what I want to do, what my desires tell me I want to do, which always seem to lead me astray."[4] Dorothy prayed for understanding, and before she knew it, she was home.

Some time later Dorothy and Forster went rowing in the bay. The smell of the sea and the cry of the gulls piqued her senses. She studied Forster's frame as he pulled the oars. How she loved him and wished she could share with him the wonder of God's presence.

Far out from shore the oyster boats bobbed on the horizon. "Look, Forster," said Dorothy, "at that ship out there with four masts. If you keep looking at it, it looks as if there are holes in its side. You can see the blue sky right through them. And it looks like the other ships are sailing along in the air instead of sitting on the horizon."[5]

Forster proceeded to explain the principles of mirages and atmospheric conditions that made the ships look as they did. Dorothy was thoughtful for a moment, then pointed out how our senses often lie to us. Immediately Forster clammed up and refused to discuss the phenomena further because it came too close to matters of faith.

Forster continued to be uneasy over Dorothy's restless search for a religious faith. He wanted to live in the love of the moment and was very jealous over any other love in her life that he suspected might come between the two of them. She, on the other hand, could not see that love between a man and woman was incompatible with the love of God. God was their Creator, and soon there was to be a child born from their union. Didn't that make them cocreators with God?

The tension increased as Dorothy progressed in her pregnancy. Forster withdrew and spent his time digging for clams, fishing on the bay, or caring for the garden. He continually reminded Dorothy that their relationship was a comradeship, not a marriage. He did not want to be shackled by repressive bonds of a legal arrangement.

Dorothy finally moved from the country into town temporarily, and her sister came to stay with her until the baby was born. Being close to friends and a church where she could go to pray sustained her. She read books of inspiration and became more determined than ever to have her child baptized. "I am not going to have my child flounder through many years as I have done, doubting and hesitating, undisciplined and amoral. I feel that it is the greatest thing I can do for my child."[6]

For herself, Dorothy prayed for the gift of faith. Should she make that final leap? She knew the cost. Forster would leave her if she embraced the church, and she would face life alone.

At last her daughter, Tamar Teresa, was born. Joy overwhelmed Dorothy until the tide of love spilled over and needed an outlet. "The final object of this love and gratitude was God," said Dorothy in retrospect. "No human being could receive or contain so vast a flood of love and joy as I often felt after the birth of my child. With this came the need to worship, to adore."[7]

She pondered the words of friends who said they did not need the church in order to worship. But Dorothy did not agree. "My very experience as a radical," she said, "my whole make-up, led me to want to associate myself with others, with the masses, in loving and praising God."[8]

The choice to travel this high road was not taken lightly. "One of the disconcerting facts about the spiritual life," Dorothy said, "is that God takes you at your word. Sooner or later you are given a chance to prove your love."[9] That chance was soon to come.

Dorothy finally took Tamar Teresa to be baptized into the Catholic faith, but she was not yet ready to make that decision for herself. The pain of separating from Forster intensified when she saw how he delighted in the baby. The inner turmoil over choosing between Forster and the church made Dorothy so ill that she knew she could not put off her decision any longer.

At last she went alone and was baptized. Many of her friends believed that by choosing this rite, she had turned her back on the cause of justice. But was choosing God a choice against justice and the poor? Didn't Jesus himself walk among the poor and powerless?

"I loved the Church for Christ made visible," Dorothy said. "Not for itself, because it was so often a scandal to me."[10]

"I felt keenly that God was more on the side of the hungry, the ragged, the unemployed, than on the side of the comfortable churchgoer who gave so little heed to the misery of the needy and the groaning of the poor. I had prayed that some way would open up for me to do something, to line myself up on their side, to work for them, so that I would no longer feel that I had been false to them in embracing my new-found faith."[11]

After Dorothy's separation from Forster, she struggled for five years with the big question of what God wanted her to do with her life. While she was working as a reporter for *The Commonweal,* a Catholic publication, her supervisor sent her to Washington, D.C., to cover an assignment and participate in a hunger march. In spite of her hectic schedule, she found time to meditate in a shrine. "God, show me how to make my life count," she begged, little suspecting that her prayer was about to be answered sooner than expected.

The eight-hour bus ride back to New York City exhausted her. She reached the apartment that she shared with her little daughter, her brother John, and his wife Teresa, eager to relax and visit with her family. But an unwelcome guest was waiting for her. His name was Peter Maurin, a man who considered himself a missionary to the world. Ever-hospitable Teresa had let him in.

Peter looked as though he had slept in his wrinkled, baggy suit. He wore heavy shoes, a stained hat, and glasses with bent frames. He knew of Dorothy's newspaper experience and had read her articles, so he hoped to interest her in the three ideas that were driving his life. With hardly an introduction he launched into a lengthy lecture.

Peter first talked about finding a way to encourage round-table discussions of social issues, highlighting the problems of poor people, perhaps in a newspaper.

Without pausing for breath, Peter explained his second hope of establishing houses of hospitality "to give the rich a chance to help the poor." A third goal was to found independent farming communes where people could meet their basic needs and have some control over their own lives.

The time for such organizations was ripe. It was 1933 and the Great Depression was in full swing. Every fifth adult American was unemployed. Factories had shut down. Mortgages on farms were being foreclosed. Hoards of people were moving into New York City to look for work. Relief and breadlines were multiplying.

Peter declared that such problems existed because people worshiped money instead of God. The solution, he said, was to take Jesus' words literally and make a personal commitment to feed the hungry, clothe the naked, and provide shelter for the homeless. He believed Christians should not think in terms of what the state or church should do, but what they, themselves could do.

Peter lived his beliefs. He shared the little he had. If someone needed a coat, he gave them his. If he had already given away his own, he begged a coat from a friend for the needy one. "I am a personalist," he said. "A personalist is a go-giver, not a go-getter. He tries to give what he has instead of trying to get what the other fellow has."[12]

As Dorothy listened to Peter, she grew excited. Not many hours ago she had begged God to help her find a way to make her life count. Writing in a newspaper would give her a vehicle through which she could expose the evils of social injustice and encourage the way of life taught by Jesus. "But how can we fund such projects?" she asked Peter.

"One never needs any money to start a good work," Peter said. "It is people who are important. If they are willing to give their work— that is the thing. God is not to be outdone in generosity. The funds will come in somehow or other."[13]

Dorothy weighed her knowledge of charitable institutions. Most of those she knew started with humble beginnings. Didn't she have a typewriter, a kitchen table, lots of paper, and plenty to write about? What more was needed?

From this simple beginning the first issue of the *Catholic Worker* was printed in May of 1933 and sold 2,500 copies. By 1936 this monthly magazine had increased its circulation to 150,000. Soon the *Catholic Worker* grew into a sweeping movement in the United States and Canada which established independent houses of hospitality and provided millions of meals for the hungry and shelter for thousands of homeless. Of the farming communes, some were more successful than others, although none met Peter's expectations.

Workers in the movement lived simply and shared what they had with those in need. Dorothy insisted that hospitality meant more than opening a door and offering a meal or bed. It meant opening one's heart to the needy as well. Her sister-in-law's mother said it well. "There's always room for one more. Everyone just take a little less."

The *Catholic Worker* movement also took a strict pacifistic position during the war and engaged in nonviolent demonstrations. Dorothy agonized over the issues to be faced during warfare. "Can there be a just war?" she asked. "What does God want me to do? And what am I capable of doing? Can I stand out against state and church? Is it pride, presumption, to think I have the spiritual capacity to use spiritual weapons in the face of the most gigantic tyranny the world has ever seen? Am I capable of enduring suffering, facing martyrdom?"[14]

Dorothy and her coworkers were jailed a number of times for their nonviolent antiwar demonstrations. Many people were suspicious of the *Catholic Worker* movement, including the F.B.I., which had a thick file on its activities.

In spite of harassment and persecution, Dorothy said, "We reaffirm our belief in the ultimate victory of good over evil, of love over hatred and we believe that the trials which beset us in the world today are for the perfecting of our faith."[15]

Writer-editor, Robert Ellsberg, said of Dorothy Day, "Yet it was not what Dorothy Day wrote that was extraordinary, nor even what she believed, but the fact that there was absolutely no distinction between what she believed, what she wrote, and the manner in which she lived."[16]

Today the *Catholic Worker* movement is still active and growing to meet the increasing needs of society. The movement is dedicated to sheltering the homeless, feeding the hungry, visiting prisoners, clothing the needy, and carrying out other acts of mercy as directed by Jesus in Matthew 25.

There are about one hundred *Catholic Worker* communities throughout the nation and half a dozen in other countries. All are outgrowths of Dorothy

Day's original community. Each one is independent and decides for itself what it feels called to do.

One such group is the Dorothy Day Center in St. Paul, Minnesota. The center furnishes a safe place for needy people to experience comfort, belonging, and the opportunity to socialize in an environment that affirms their dignity and self-worth. The center also helps those who are homeless, ill, or drug addicted. It provides personal items, a food shelf, medical assistance, and practical services such as maintaining a place for individuals to pick up their mail, wash and dry clothes, and receive counseling.

Notes

1. Hugh T. Kerr and John M. Mulder, eds., "Dorothy Day" in *Conversions* (Grand Rapids: William B. Eerdmans, 1983), 211.

2. Dorothy Day, *The Long Loneliness* (New York: Harper & Brothers, Publishers, 1952), 133.

3. Ibid., 445.

4. Robert Ellsberg, ed., *By Little and By Little, The Selected Writings of Dorothy Day* (New York: Alfred A. Knopf, 1984), xxiii.

5. Kerr and Mulder, "Dorothy Day," 212.

6. Ibid., 213.

7. Day, *The Long Loneliness*, 139.

8. Ibid., 139.

9. Ibid., 139.

10. Ibid., 149–150.

11. Dorothy Day, *Loaves and Fishes* (New York: Harper & Row, Publishers, 1963), 13.

12. Ibid., 21.

13. Ibid., 10.

14. Day, *The Long Loneliness*, 272–273.

15. Dorothy Day, *A Harsh and Dreadful Love* (New York: Liveright, 1973), 306.

16. Ellsberg, *By Little*, Introduction, xv.

17 *Sadhu Sundar Singh*

1889–ca. 1929

"Isn't there any peace to be found in this life?" Sundar Singh wailed. "I've done everything I know how to do. I rise early to read our sacred scriptures. I pray. I meditate late into the night, and I practice yoga, yet I can find no peace."

Sundar's father, Sher Singh, looked at his agitated, fifteen-year-old son. "Boys of your age think of nothing but games and play," he said, "but how has this mania possessed you at so early an age? There is plenty of time to think of these things later in life. I suppose you must have gotten this madness from your mother and the Sadhu."[1]

A painful memory gripped Sundar's heart: his gentle mother. Why did she have to die? She was the one who encouraged him to meditate and pray, and to study. When he was young, she had arranged for a sadhu, a holy man, to instruct him, hoping that someday he would become a sadhu also.

Sundar remembered a recent discussion with his Hindu teacher. "Sundar," he said, "you must play more and not be so serious. You will understand the true meaning of these truths when you are older."

"If a hungry boy asked you for bread, would you tell him to go and play?" asked Sundar. "Would you tell him to wait until he was grown up so he could understand the real meaning of hunger? I am hungry for spiritual bread now. If you do not know where I can get it, then say so."[2]

"If your hunger is not satisfied in this life, it will be in your next re-births, provided you keep on trying," his teacher answered.

Re-birth. Sundar wondered what form his mother would take as she was reborn into this life. Would he recognize her? He couldn't bear not seeing her ever again.

Sundar thought of the strange ideas he had read in the Bible at the mission school that he attended in Rampur. He was sure no one could ever make a Christian out of him!

One day Sundar burst into the house after throwing stones at the missionaries. He was carrying a Bible. "I won't have them teaching me about their foreign God," he raved to his father. He tore the Bible into pieces and threw them into the fire. "I will never be a Christian! Never!"

Calmly Sher Singh said, "My son, think of the fine education you have been receiving from the missionaries. Appreciate that and ignore their religious teachings. We have wisdom from our own holy books to live by."

Sundar's unrest grew daily. In spite of his hatred for Christianity, there was something compelling about the foreign God—a God who entered the lives of ordinary people, a God who loved, forgave, and gave the world his own Son. Could such a God exchange his own despair for peace?

Sundar was so distressed that he finally locked himself in his room. Why was he so troubled? Wasn't he a Sikh, a person of high birth who belonged to a proud and noble people? He had wealth and a beautiful home set among the splendid landscape of northern India. What wrenched his heart in this manner? Was it his mother's death? Partly, perhaps. But it was more than that. There was a deep longing inside him for a God who could take away the darkness he felt in his soul.

The third night after burning the Bible, Sundar rose at 3:00 A.M. to worship. After a ritual cold bath, he began to pray. "If there is a God at all," he pleaded, "reveal yourself to me. Show me the way of salvation and end this unrest of my soul, or I will throw myself under the morning railway train."[3]

Sundar continued to pray, expecting to see Krishna, or Buddha, or some other Hindu god. But then a light began to shine in the room. Brighter and brighter it grew until within a globe of light there appeared the form of the living Christ. Never had Sundar seen such a glorious and loving face. Christ spoke to Sundar in his own language. "Why do you persecute me? See, I have died on the cross for you and for the whole world."[4] Sundar fell before Jesus and vowed to be his follower and serve him forever. His heart was filled with inexpressible joy and peace.

After he told his family and relatives about his experience, they all tried to talk Sundar out of this new nonsense, but there was no dissuading the young man, even with promises of great rewards. Finally he was disowned by his kin and ordered to leave home. They prepared poisoned food for him to eat on the journey, hoping that once he was dead he would no longer disgrace the family. Half-dead, he struggled to the mission school where loving people nursed him back to health.

The day he was baptized, intense joy mended the pain of persecution. Now Sundar knew he belonged to Christ, a vessel for his use. He said, "The whole universe was like a great ocean of joy. I felt myself drowning in sweetness."[5]

After completing years of study at school, Sundar chose to be a sadhu, a simple holy man, rather than an ordained minister. He began walking from village to village preaching new life in Christ and serving wherever he found a need. He was tall, young, and handsome, and delivered his message with the "fire of a prophet and the power of an apostle," reported a Madras newspaper.

People were drawn to his gentle manners and his beautiful smile. One Hindu teacher said that from the moment he saw Sundar, he could see by his face that Sundar had realized the bliss which he himself had been struggling to find.

Sundar never sought fame but within a few years this mystical man who frequently saw visions was becoming known all over India and in other parts of the world. Invitations for speaking engagements poured in from many places. Sundar was rushed from place to place where he saw people worshiping materialism instead of Christ, feeding their brains with great learning but starving their souls, Christians seeking power for themselves rather than power over sin, quarreling factions too busy for prayer. Willingly he went, but how the crowds exhausted him. He preferred a simple life of service and ministry.

In spite of his popularity, there were localities where Sadhu Sundar Singh was reviled and persecuted. In Nepal his opponents clamped him naked into stocks, and dumped a basket of leeches over his body. Through his misery he continued to preach and sing praises to God.

Some of his hearers went to the governor. "What's the use of putting this sadhu in prison?" they asked. "When he was preaching, no one took notice of him, and but now that he is in prison, the people flock to hear him."

"Let him out," the governor said. "He is mad." So Sundar was released.

Before Sundar left the village, a man who had torn up St. Mark's Gospel while he was also imprisoned asked, "Can a madman be so happy? If a madman has such joy then I should like to be mad too, and not only I, but also the whole world."[6] He asked for forgiveness and later was baptized.

One part of the world that drew Sundar like a magnet was wind-swept Tibet on the roof of the world. No one could persuade him to avoid the risks of that forbidding land. As he set out once again on his yearly trek, anxiety tugged at the hearts of his friends. Would he come back this time?

Up and up the steep trail of the mighty mountains of Himalaya Sundar trudged. He made his way along narrow ledges, across rickety bridges, and through howling gales and blinding snow in high mountain passes. One misstep might mean a fall into deep chasms below.

Sadhu Sundar Singh remembered various welcomes he had received from the villagers when he traveled here before. More than once angry mobs had stoned him. He had been beaten, tied to a tree, and tormented in other ways for daring to preach the Christian gospel.

The snow was picking up. Sundar recalled the last time he had walked this rugged way with a companion and stumbled on a half-frozen man lying in the snow. "We can't stop," said Sundar's companion. "We'll be lucky to save ourselves." And he went his way. Sundar tended the man, then hoisted him on his back. As he carried him through the storm, the exertion warmed his own body and gave heat to the victim. Before they reached their destination, they found Sundar's companion lying in the snow, dead. The scene brought back Christ's words, "Those who want to save their life will lose it, and those who lose their life for my sake will find it."[7]

At last Sundar arrived at the village of Risar, beyond Kailash Mountain. As he began to preach, a crowd pushed about him. After talking about the gift of salvation through Jesus Christ, someone asked, "How is it possible that by the death of one man others can be saved?"

Sadhu Sundar Singh told of a man whose son lay near death. The doctor said, "Unless your son receives blood, he will die. And I have none to give him."

"I will give him my blood," said the father. Because he was an old man, he died giving his blood, but his son's life was saved.

"This is how Jesus has saved us," said Sundar.[8]

"Tell us another story," the people begged. So Sundar told about a man who had a flock of sheep. Every morning the servants took the sheep to graze on the mountainside. But one night some of the sheep failed to come home. "Go find my sheep," said the owner. But the servants were afraid of the night and the wild animals, so they refused to go. "If I go as myself," the owner said, "the sheep will not follow because they do not know me. So I must become like a sheep." He put on a sheepskin and went out into the night. He searched until he found the lost and bleating sheep, and they followed him home.

Sundar told them that this was what God did for lost people, too. He said, "God clothed Himself in the robe of our humanity so that He would be like us, and we would not be afraid of Him."[9]

Soon the Buddhist lamas got wind of Sundar's return. "It is dangerous to let this stranger come to our country and fill our people with false ideas," said one. "He may lead our people astray and they won't listen to us anymore."

"We have only one choice," said the chief lama, and he whispered his plan.

Sadhu Sundar Singh was arrested and brought before the authorities. "What do you mean by preaching this Jesus Christ?" they asked.

"I must obey my Master," answered Sundar.

"We have nothing to do with your Master," said the chief. You must promise not to preach."

"I cannot promise," Sundar answered.

"Then throw him in the well!" commanded the leader. Sundar Singh was dragged over stony paths to a well on the outskirts of town. His captors broke his left arm before unlocking and removing a heavy iron cover on the well. Then they pushed Sundar over the edge. As he landed at the bottom, he heard the heavy lid clang shut above him. A key turned in the lock.

The foul stench nearly overcame Sundar as he tried to raise himself. Horrors! His flesh crawled as he pushed against something soft and yielding. Dead and decaying bodies! "Help me, oh God," he cried out. "Must I die like this, alone in this terrible place!" How long will it take? he wondered. Hours? Days? Weeks of pain, rotting flesh, slow suffocation, thirst, hunger, darkness!

As Sundar drifted in and out of consciousness, wisps of memory floated across his pain: his mother, father, home, green hills, quiet forests. Yet he would never exchange the present horror for his life of luxury before he had faith in Christ when he had had such agony of soul. God's joy made up for all hardships. Now as he faced death, he felt as if he were about to step from a darkened room into one filled with peace and light. Was it day or night? One, two, or three days? He had lost all track of time.

Suddenly there was a noise above him. A key turned in the lock. The heavy lid was lifted off the well and Sundar could see the stars above! Fresh air rushed to his senses. He saw the outline of a man in the darkness. A voice whispered, "Hold fast to this rope." The rope was lowered and Sundar grasped hold with every ounce of strength in his failing and pain-filled body. The man drew him up and up. Then Sundar collapsed unconscious, at the top. When he recovered, his arm was healed and there was no one in sight.

With wonder, Sundar gave thanks to God as he made his way to friends in the village who first believed he was a ghost. When he began to preach again, the furious lamas demanded an answer. "How did you escape from the well?"

Sundar recounted his story. "Who set you free?" the lamas persisted.

"I do not know," answered Sundar. "It was too dark to see his face."

"Someone must have stolen my key," stormed the chief lama. "Search each person here and find the guilty person."

No key turned up during the search. Then the leader lifted the bunch of keys that hung on his waist, and he paled. There hung the key, on his own girdle.

"Go away from us, holy man," he begged. "Your God is terrible and powerful. Leave us alone lest some harm come on all of us."

Sadhu Sundar Singh wanted to tell the lamas about the love and peace of the living Christ. But they were all so terrified that they were in no mind to listen, so Sundar went his way.

After he returned to India, calls were waiting from Ceylon, Burma, Japan, Europe, England, America, Scandinavia, and many other places, begging him to come. As he prepared to travel, an urgent message came from his father with whom he had had no contact for many years. The reunion was especially joyful, because Sundar's father was now a Christian and wanted to spend his riches financing his son's trips.

Sundar traveled until his health failed. Then he retired to writing for several years. But once again came that inner call to Tibet. Sundar set his face toward the heights, and cheerfully promised his friends he would be back by summer. He never returned. No one knows what happened to him. For years, people waited, hoped, and searched, but they finally accepted that Sundar had taken his last journey, home to be with the Lord.

Notes

1. Sadhu Sundar Singh, *With and Without Christ* (Madras: Christian Literature Society, 1969), 51.
2. Ibid., 52.
3. Ibid., 56.
4. Ibid., 56.
5. T. E. Riddle, *The Vision and the Call* (Kharar, Punjab, India: First Indian edition, 1964), 19.
6. Sadhu Sundar Singh, *Life in Abundance*, sermons recorded by Alys Goodwin (Switzerland: Christian Literature Society, 1986), 3.
7. Matthew 16:25 NRSV.
8. Singh, *Life in Abundance*, 33–34.
9. Ibid., 27–28.

18 Tariri (tah-ree-ree) Nóchomata Yatarisá b. ca. 1915

Tariri, great chief of the Shapra people, could not sleep. He tossed and turned on his platform bed under his palm thatch roof in the Peruvian jungle. His mind struggled with the changes that were tearing his restless spirit apart. He was known as a fearless killer. The hatred and anger that burned within his heart had always given him the courage he needed to kill his enemies, then to take their heads and shrink them. He had many fine heads in his collection.

He had learned the art of killing from his father. At age ten he was taught how to spear the dying enemies so he would lose his fear of bloodshed. "If I should die while I am out killing," his father told him, "do not throw away my words but keep them in your heart."[1] Now new words were troubling Chief Tariri.

The confusion all started some months ago when Victorino, the Peruvian rubber trader from down on the big river, asked him if two white women could come to live among his people.

"Why do the women want to live here?" Tariri asked. "Are they looking for husbands?"

"They want to learn your language and teach you about their God," answered Victorino. "And they have medicine to help you when you are sick."

Chief Tariri asked himself, "Why would these women come all this way to teach the Shapra people something unless it was extremely important?" Somehow he felt that good might be in store for his community. "Let them come," he announced.

"Then build them a house," said Victorino, handing Chief Tariri lots of cloth and many shirts. "This is payment for the house. They will give you more when it is finished. Tariri promised to look after the women as he would his own sisters.

As Chief Tariri worked on the house, Old Shotka, the upriver chief warned him, "First the women come. The foreign men will follow and they will kill you. If these women were men, I would kill them right now." Others agreed. The tribal women were angry, too, because they were afraid the foreigners would compete for their husbands.

"I say they are to come," said Chief Tariri, and since his word was law, it stood.

The house was ready the day the *kirinkos* (Americans) arrived in their flying canoes (float planes). "What if they put the Shapra people in those canoes, take us away from our land, and make us work for them?" worried Tariri. He stared as the white women descended from the planes. In their long dresses they reminded him of *shoroshoro* birds with long, flowing feathers.

Although Tariri was a bit apprehensive, he felt sorry for the women. They were far from their families, and they couldn't even talk! They stumbled over the few Candoshi-Shapra words they knew. Yes, they needed help. He named them Monchanki (Lorrie Doris Anderson) and Mpawachi (Doris Cox) after his sisters.

Tariri felt proud to teach the missionaries his language. Little by little they learned enough words to tell Tariri that a powerful God made the world and everything in it. They showed him a book that told about this great God who loved him. The book told about God's Son, Jesus, and taught that it was wrong to kill others.

Hearing all these words about God made Tariri's heart strangely happy, but at the same time the words made him all mixed up. He needed to think about them for a while because he and his people believed in witch doctors and in many spirits. They especially feared the spirit of the great anaconda (water boa) which lived in deep and watery places. When someone was sick, Tariri chanted to the spirit of the anaconda, challenging it to let go of the sick person's soul. If that person died, it meant that the anaconda had won.

All these thoughts tumbled through Chief Tariri's mind as he reviewed the past events. Finally he fell into a fitful sleep. In his dreams the new teachings mingled with the old, pulling him this way and that.

Over the next months, Tariri continued to teach Mpawachi and Monchanki the Candoshi-Shapra language. Meanwhile he was learning story after story about Jesus and his amazing teachings. When Tariri heard the very first Bible verse translated into his own language, he said excitedly, "When you talk like that, my heart leaps with understanding."[2]

After a few years Doris Cox went back to the U.S. for a furlough, and Rachel Saint came to study the language and be Lorrie's partner. Chief Tariri named her Tiyotari.

Although Tariri learned quickly, he was still torn between the new and old ideas. Could he still be a powerful chief if he did not kill? Was God really greater than the anaconda? Was it true that God loved even his enemies upriver?

One day a mother brought her baby to Lorrie and Rachel. The child was deathly sick and burning with fever. His eyes had rolled back in his head, and he appeared to be in a coma as convulsions racked his little body. The anguished mother wanted Tariri to chant to the spirit of the anaconda so it would release its death grip on her baby. If the chanting didn't work, Monchanki and Tiyotari could treat the child.

Lorrie could see instantly that it would take more than medicine to cure this baby. "There can be no delay," she said to the mother with a worried frown. "We must get the fever down immediately. Let us treat your baby and pray to our God." But the mother was afraid to anger the spirits. "Tariri must chant!" she wailed.

Since God's power was at stake, Lorrie and Rachel went to Tariri who was already chanting behind his mosquito net. "God's Word says we cannot mix witch doctoring with the worship of our God," said the women.

Tariri hedged. Wasn't he Chief of the Seven Rivers? Didn't his people depend on him to challenge the power of the anaconda? If he did not do so, and the baby died, then what? Yet, he remembered how his wife, Irina, had recovered when his white sisters prayed to their God. Reluctantly he agreed.

The anxious mother watched Lorrie and Rachel sponge her baby with tepid water and give him aspirin. She listened as they pleaded with their God to spare the ebbing life of her child.

All of a sudden the baby opened his eyes! A beautiful smile lit his face, and he began to play. Like lightning, word spread around the village. "The power of God is greater than the power of the anaconda!"

Every now and then the missionaries flew back to Yarinachocha for a short break. One day when they returned, Chief Tariri was preparing for a big fiesta at his home. From the *yuca* root his wife had fermented plenty of *masato* to serve his guests. In the midst of fiesta arrangements, the chief began feeling sick. His bones ached and he burned with fever, yet he welcomed his guests and began the feasting and drinking. All night the party continued while the men consumed more and more *masato*. Soon their talking and arguing grew so rowdy that the women and children ran and hid before the machetes began clanging and bullets started to fly.

In the morning Chief Tariri felt worse. He dragged himself over to see Tiyotari and Monchanki. "I must go see a very strong witch doctor," he groaned.

Lorrie said, "If you do that, you will be throwing away God's Word." Again Tariri felt the clash of two cultures. He was powerfully drawn to the great God over all, yet he was afraid to anger the spirit of the mighty anaconda.

"I will be back in five sleeps," he said, then added, "Perhaps if I could read God's Word for myself, I would not go." Then Tariri set off in a canoe, sheltered by a palm leaf.

From the chief's remark, Lorrie and Rachel realized more than ever the urgency of translating God's Word into the Candoshi-Shapra language so the people could read it themselves and feel it was their own. As Lorrie tackled the Gospels, Rachel worked with Tsirimpo, Tariri's teenage son, translating simple stories for the children.

After Chief Tariri's return, he labored with Lorrie every evening as together they translated the stories of Jesus. Each day he repeated the latest story to the men as they all worked.

Day after day, Lorrie worked with the texts, through the heat and through bouts of fever. Soon the chief knew stories about Jesus speaking to the wind and water, Jesus healing Lazarus, Jesus making the blind see, and stories about Jesus' death and resurrection. When Tariri learned the passion story, he was so impressed that he invited his friend, Shimpotka, to come hear it.

Shimpotka came in his feathers and paint and brought others to listen. Tariri sat cross-legged on his chief's platform, wearing a regal crown of toucan feathers. His shiny, black hair hung about his shoulders. Excitedly gesturing with his hands, Chief Tariri told his guests the story.

As Tariri learned more from the Gospels, he discovered that he was beginning to love Jesus. Who else was like him? Who else could do the things he did?

When Doris Cox returned from her furlough, Rachel told Tariri that she was leaving to take God's Word to the Auca Indians (now called Waorani). Tariri felt sad. "We loved Tiyotari very much," he said. "Of course she went because God ordered her to go . . . she has a heart like a chief. Being strong, she went."[3]

As Lorrie completed new Bible stories, Chief Tariri recorded them in his language. In his own words he added, "When we, in a long time, throw out the witch doctors, we will tell our children it is because our sisters came and taught us that Jesus is greater."[4]

When Tariri learned what God's Word said about lying, stealing, hating, and killing, he described the consequences of such actions. "God will put those who kill into darkness. One's eyes unable to see will always make one lose the way. . . . It is terrible to be lost like that. That is where the people who do not love God will live."[5]

One day Chief Tariri went hunting. On his way home he struggled with the questions that had been troubling him over the past few years. "What do I want to do with my life? I want to be greater than all people. . . . Then everybody will fear me and I will be happy. I want to live by myself with nobody to bother. I should have killed everyone. . . . Without anyone around, who would care what one did?" Suddenly he stopped. "What am I saying?" he asked himself. "This is what I will do. I will love God."[6]

Tariri arrived home from the hunt covered with dirt, sweat, and monkey blood. Mpawachi called to him. He threw down his blowgun, his dartholder still over his shoulder. "When are you going to receive Jesus into your life?" she asked.

Tariri was ready. He had thought about this moment for a long time. With joy he answered, "I want very much to receive Jesus into my heart, Mpawachi. I will not say, 'no,' at all."[7]

Then Tariri prayed, "Jesus, you cleanse me with your blood. Put good in my heart. . . . Throw all the dirt away. I will follow only you. . . . I do not want to live bad any more."[8] Tariri was aware that he badly needed a bath on the outside, but he knew that he was now washed clean on the inside.

When Chief Tariri told everyone about his new heart, his family and neighbors wanted to know more about Jesus too. From then on Tariri could be heard praying to God before meals and every night before going to sleep. He knew there would be many struggles, and that he would need strength from God to prevent him from being pulled back into the old ways.

At night, lying in bed, listening to the owl and the frogs, he would think to himself. "I have now received Jesus. Having done that, what shall I do? Shall I live right? Yes, I will.

"Before I did not worry about being bad. . . . Like a wild boar that rolls in the dirt and gets dirty all over, that is what I was like. I rest my heart in God now. Why should we not love Him?"[9]

Tariri faced many times of testing in his new faith. When two of his sons died, friends said, "That is what you get for loving God. Look at us. Even though we get drunk, our children do not die. . . . It is not worth it to follow God."[10]

Although the chief cried much for his sons, he remembered Job who lost children through death. "He did not leave God," said Tariri. "He did not throw God's Word away. Why should I?"[11] There were more trials, illnesses, and life-threatening accidents. Yet Tariri did not throw away God's words. "We cannot live without Him," he declared. "We would be like fish drunk with barbasco root, not knowing where we are going."[12]

When the upriver people deceived Chief Tariri, killed his brother-in-law, and nearly killed him, he surprised them all. In the old days he would have taken revenge. Now his enemies discovered that because Tariri loved God, he did not pay back evil for evil. He did not beat his wife anymore, or get drunk, talk bad, and fight. "It is as if there were no Tariri," they said.

As Chief Tariri taught his children he reminded them, "Ask God to help you when you work. Do not just go out . . . and not even think about God. Ask before you go."[13]

After his conversion, opportunities opened up for Tariri to travel outside his tribe. With dignity and poise he spoke eloquently at important conferences and gatherings in the capital city, Lima, and other places. Besides explaining the deep desire of his people for education, he couldn't help but tell about his new heart. When he spoke to an assembly of students he told them, "I feel that every man is my brother, every woman my sister, and every child my son or daughter. Do not leave the path planned by God."[14]

When he and Irina visited the United States, the embarrassed newspaper reporters couldn't stop Tariri from talking about Jesus at every opportunity.

Because Chief Tariri did not throw away God's Word, people in places near and far, including many former enemies, came to know Christ and the power of his resurrection. He became a stabilizing influence for the whole tribe, and has been frequently called upon to act as a liaison between feuding parties. He has been the peacemaker for the entire Shapra area.

One thing Chief Tariri regrets is that it took so long for the missionaries to come. "If you had told us long ago, the old ones would have known it, too. Nevertheless, we praise God. Before you came, all was darkness. Now there is light."[15]

Notes

1. Tariri (as told to Ethel Emily Wallis), *Tariri, My Story* (New York: Harper & Row, Publishers, 1965), 36.
2. Ibid., 73.
3. Ibid., 68.
4. Ibid., 69.
5. Ibid., 70.
6. Ibid., 71.
7. Ibid., 73.
8. Ibid., 72.
9. Ibid., 75.
10. Ibid., 85.
11. Ibid., 86.
12. Ibid., 89.
13. Ibid., 91.
14. Ibid., 99–100.
15. Robert Griffin, ed., "I'd Do It Again If I Could!" Vol. 17, Number 2, March/April 1989 of BEYOND (Waxhaw, N.C.: JAARS, 1989).

For Further Reading

Addams, Jane. *Twenty Years at Hull-House with Autobiographical Notes*. New York: The Macmillan Company, 1939.

Bell, Ken, and Henriette Major. *A Man and His Mission: Cardinal Léger in Africa*. Scarborough, Ontario: Prentice-Hall, 1976.

Bishop, Edward. *Blood and Fire! The Story of General William Booth and The Salvation Army*. London: Longmans, Green and Co., 1964.

Bradford, Sarah. *Harriet Tubman, The Moses of Her People*. New York: Corinth Books, 1961.

Carlson, Carole C. *Corrie ten Boom: Her Life and Faith*. Old Tappan, N.J.: Fleming H. Revell Company, 1983.

Collier, Richard. *The General Next to God: The Story of William Booth and The Salvation Army*. New York: E. P. Dutton & Co., 1965.

Conrad, Earl. *Harriet Tubman: A Biography by Earl Conrad*. New York: Paul S. Eriksson, 1943.

Davey, Cyril J. *Kagawa of Japan*. New York: Abingdon Press, 1960.

———. *The Yellow Robe: The Story of Sadhu Sundar Singh*. London: The Camelot Press Ltd., 1950.

Davids, Richard C. *The Man Who Moved a Mountain*. Philadelphia: Fortress Press, 1970.

Day, Dorothy. *By Little and By Little: The Selected Writings of Dorothy Day*. Edited by Robert Ellsberg. New York: Alfred A. Knopf, 1984.

———. *A Harsh and Dreadful Love*. New York: Liveright, 1973.

———. *The Long Loneliness: The Autobiography of Dorothy Day*. New York: Harper & Brothers, 1952.

————. *Loaves and Fishes*. New York: Harper & Row, 1963.

Duggan, James. *Paul-Émile Léger*. Don Mills, Ontario: Fitzhenry and Whiteside Limited, 1981.

Elliott, Lawrence. *George Washington Carver: The Man Who Overcame*. Englewood Cliffs, N.J.: Prentice-Hall, Inc., 1966.

Fairbank, Jenty. *William and Catherine Booth: God's Soldiers*. London: Hodder and Stoughton, 1974.

Harris, J. Henry, Editor. *Robert Raikes: The Man and His Work*. New York: E. P. Dutton, n.d. (Bristol, England: J. W. Arrowsmith).

Hill, Harvey Jay. *He Heard God's Whisper: A Story of Dr. Geo. W. Carver*. Minneapolis: Jorgenson Press, 1943.

Holt, Rackham. *George Washington Carver: An American Biography*. Garden City: Doubleday, Doran and Company, Inc., 1944.

Kerr, Hugh T., and John M. Mulder, Editors. *Conversions: The Christian Experience*. Grand Rapids, Mich.: William B. Eerdmans Publishing Company, 1983.

Laubach, Frank C. *Letters By a Modern Mystic*. New York: Student Volunteer Movement, 1937.

Lukesh, Chas., Translator from Russian into English. *"Greasy," The Robber*. Minneapolis: Osterhus Publishing Company, 1942.

Medary, Marjorie. *Each One Teach One: Frank Laubach, Friend to Millions*. New York: David McKay Company, Inc., 1954.

Miller, Basil. *George Washington Carver: God's Ebony Scientist*. Grand Rapids, Mich., 1953.

Nathan, Dorothy. *Women of Courage*. New York: Random House, 1964.

Parkman, Mary R. *Heroines of Service*. New York: The Century Co., 1917.

Petry, Ann. *Harriet Tubman: Conductor on the Underground Railroad*. New York: Pocket Books, a Simon & Schuster division of Gulf and Western Corporation, 1955.

Riddle, T. E. *The Vision and the Call: A Life of Sadhu Sundar Singh*. Kharar, Punjab, India: First Indian edition, 1964.

Roberts, Helen M. *Champion of The Silent Billion: The Story of Frank C. Laubach, Apostle of Literacy*. St. Paul: Macalester Park Publishing Company, 1961.

Rose, June. *Elizabeth Fry: A Biography*. New York: St. Martin's Press, 1980.

Sandvik, Marie, and Doris Nye. *To the Slums with Love*. Minneapolis: Marie Sandvik Center, 1976.

Schildgen, Robert. *Toyohiko Kagawa: Apostle of Love and Social Justice*. Berkeley: Centenary Books, 1988. American Committee for The Kagawa Centennial Project, 1988.

Singh, Sadhu Sundar. *At the Master's Feet*. Madras, India: The Christian Literature Society, 1921.

————. *The Cross Is Heaven: The Life and Writings of Sadhu Sundar Singh*. Edited by A. J. Appasamy, D. Phil., D.D. London: United Society for Christian Literature, Lutterworth Press, 1956.

————. *Life in Abundance.* (Sermons of the Sadhu recorded by Alys Goodwin in Switzerland, March 1922. Edited by A. F. Thyagaraju) Christian Literature Society, 1986.

————. *The Real Life.* Madras, India: The Christian Literature Society, 1965.

————. *Reality and Religion: Meditations on God, Man and Nature.* London: Macmillan & Co., 1924. Madras, India: The Christian Literature Society, 1968.

————. *The Search After Reality.* London: Macmillan & Co., Ltd., 1925. Madras, India: The Christian Literature Society, 1968.

————. *The Spiritual Life: Meditations on Various Aspects of the Spiritual Life.* London: Macmillan & Co., Ltd., 1926.

————. *With and Without Christ.* Madras, India. The Christian Literature Society, 1969.

Sterling, Dorothy. *Freedom Train: The Story of Harriet Tubman.* New York: Doubleday & Company, Inc., 1954.

Swift, Hildegarde Hoyt. *The Railroad to Freedom: A Story of the Civil War.* New York: Harcourt, Brace and Company, 1932.

Tariri. *Tariri: My Story.* (As told to Ethel Emily Wallis.) New York: Harper & Row, Publishers, 1965.

Taylor, M. W. *Harriet Tubman: Antislavery Activist.* New York: Chelsea House Publishers, 1991.

ten Boom, Corrie, with John and Elizabeth Sherrill. *The Hiding Place.* Minneapolis: World Wide Publications, 1971.

Théorêt, Chantal, Editor-in-Chief. *In Remembrance . . . 1904–1991, Cardinal Paul-Émile Léger.* Printed in Canada by Partnership Publishing, a subsidiary of the Jules and Paul-Émile Léger Foundation, 1992.

Woodham-Smith, Cecil. *Florence Nightingale.* London: McGraw-Hill Book Company, Inc., 1951.